D1286323

CAN WE BE GOOD
WITHOUT GOD?

A Conversation About Truth, Morality, Culture & a Few Other Things That Matter

Paul Chamberlain

InterVarsity Press
Downers Grove, Illinois

© 1996 by Paul Chamberlain

All rights reserved. No part of this book may be reproduced in any form without written permission from InterVarsity Press, P.O. Box 1400, Downers Grove, Illinois 60515.

InterVarsity Press® is the book-publishing division of InterVarsity Christian Fellowship®, a student movement active on campus at hundreds of universities, colleges and schools of nursing in the United States of America, and a member movement of the International Fellowship of Evangelical Students. For information about local and regional activities, write Public Relations Dept., InterVarsity Christian Fellowship, 6400 Schroeder Rd., P.O. Box 7895, Madison, WI 53707-7895.

Cover illustration: Kurt Mitchell
ISBN 0-8308-1686-0

Printed in the United States of America ∞

Library of Congress Cataloging-in-Publication Data has been requested.

17	16	15	14	13	12	11	10	9	8	7	6	5	4	3	2	1
10	09	08	07	06	05	04	03	02	01	00	99	98	97	96		

To my parents
Whether in prosperity or in adversity,
they have exemplified the moral principles
for which this book seeks a foundation.

Acknowledgments

This book arose out of a debate I participated in with a professor of philosophy from a neighboring university. The topic of the debate was the same as that of this book, and the research for that exercise formed the basis for this work.

The writing of this volume was accomplished with the help and encouragement of many people. First I wish to thank Gordon Carkner, the organizer of the aforementioned debate, who initially encouraged me to put these ideas into print. In addition, my sincere thanks go to Dr. William Lane Craig, Dr. Brian Stiller, Professor Art Chamberlain, Professor Bill Badke, Professor John Sutherland, lecturer Michael Horner, and authors Joel Freeman and Phil Callaway for reading this manuscript and making invaluable comments on both its arguments and its style. Many changes were made on the basis of these comments.

Further, I wish to acknowledge the contribution made by my adviser, John Penner, who helped develop the story line running through this book. His creativity has, I am sure, made the reading more enjoyable and the argument more relevant.

My most sincere thanks, however, are reserved for my family. They deserve high commendation for never swerving in their support of me or of this project during the time I devoted myself to it.

Introduction

We are quickly reaching a state of moral chaos in our society. *Time* magazine said it best in its cover story on "Kids, Sex & Values": "Just do it. Just say no. Just wear a condom. What's a kid supposed to think?" (May 24, 1993). Indeed. Amid the maze of conflicting messages, what is *anyone* supposed to think?

But we're faced not only with the "old" issues like sexual morality, war, racism, poverty and capital punishment. New technologies and changing perspectives are producing an avalanche of new and difficult issues, from euthanasia to genetic engineering to fetal implants to the cloning of human beings. Issues such as these demand painstaking ethical examination.

Here is the problem. Doing ethics means working from general moral principles to specific conclusions about what we ought to do. But where are these moral principles? Where are the guidelines to help us through the moral maze? It appears that at the very time we need them most, fewer of them exist for us to use. But let it be said that with no clear starting point available in the ethical task, no conclusion is possible either. We need a moral foundation.

This book comes to grips with two of the most basic questions of life and human existence. First, is there any real right and wrong (objective moral standards), the kind that does not depend on anyone's view or opinion? Second, if there are such standards, why? How can there be? What is their foundation?

These two questions are addressed in the form of a dramatic interaction among five individuals, each holding a different major viewpoint: moral relativism, atheism, secular humanism, evolution and Christian theism. Each representative spokesperson speaks his or her mind forthrightly and is continuously engaged by the others.

No attempt is made to compare these five views in a comprehensive manner. Rather, our specific concern here is limited to what each has to say on these two fundamental questions: the existence of objective moral standards and the foundation for them. Welcome to the dialogue.

The Dialogue

The Time
The present

The Place
A quiet, lavish room

The Characters
Ted the Christian
Graham the Atheist
Francine the Moral Relativist
William the Evolutionist
Ian the Secular Humanist
The Doorkeeper

The Topic
Right and Wrong

Part 1
DO REAL RIGHT &
WRONG EXIST?

Part I
DO REAL RIGHT &
WRONGS EXIST

1
WHAT'S AT STAKE?
The Meaning of Morality

Ted was apprehensive. What kind of event could this be? He reread the invitation again, but it offered no hint of who the host might be. Who would organize a party but remain anonymous?

The last line read, "A car and driver will provide transportation at 11:30 a.m. on the ninth." He glanced at his watch and looked up to see a long black limousine arrive precisely on time.

The car headed across town, but Ted was still puzzled. Who would send a car like this? Where was he going, and whom would he meet? Would he know anyone? The car turned into a drive. A gate swung open, revealing well-tended grounds and a large, stately house.

A reserved man with wire-rimmed glasses greeted him at the door and ushered him through the foyer into a reception room. He handed Theo a drink and said, "Enjoy your lunch. A car will be waiting for you at 2:00 p.m." Then he disappeared. Ted looked around: paintings, leather chairs, bookcases, foreign artifacts, large windows overlooking a garden, and a table full of food. He could see four other people. They looked as lost as he did. Was this everybody?

Cautiously he walked over to one young man and extended his hand. "My name's Theo," he introduced himself. "Theo Douglas. But please call me Ted." As he spoke, he was conscious of the young man's piercing, blue-eyed gaze, and he wondered how he would respond.

"Graham," said the young man spiritedly in a raspy voice as he grasped Ted's hand.

"Well, Graham, may I ask what brings you here?" Ted asked with a disarming smile.

"I don't know. I received this invitation, but it's unsigned. I don't know why I'm here. What brings you here?"

Ted was surprised. "Did it look like this?" He pulled out his own invitation.

"That's it, exactly!" said Graham. "So you don't know why you're here either?"

"I'm afraid not," answered Ted. "But somebody's up to something."

Suddenly Graham noticed the cross pinned to Ted's lapel. "You're not one of those religious types, are you?" he asked.

"Some would say so," Ted said casually. "I take it you're not."

"You could tell, could you?" Graham laughed. "Well, you're right. Being an atheist, I don't spend a lot of time thinking about religion. I hope that doesn't offend you."

"Not at all, but let me get this straight. You believe you can actually prove there is no God and no beyond? That is your position, isn't it? I mean, you're not simply an agnostic who claims he doesn't know?"

"You've got me straight," said Graham. "They wouldn't have elected me president of the Society for the Promotion of Atheistic Research if I weren't a true-blue atheist. SPAR is very fussy about the views of its leaders."

Ted whistled softly. "I've heard of your organization.

SPAR. And you're the president?"

"That's right. I was just elected at our annual general meeting last week, and I can see it's bothering you."

"No, of course not. It's a free country. You've got a moral right to hold any view you choose on that issue."

"How liberated! But back to my question: aren't you one of those religious types?"

"As I said, some would say so," replied Ted, "but I prefer to use different terms to refer to myself."

"Such as?"

"I prefer to call myself a Christian."

"Well now, isn't there a sense in which most of us are *Defining a* Christians, or at least have captured the essence of Chris- *Christian* tianity? Take me, for instance. I lead a decent, moral life. You know, pay my bills, treat others fairly, speak honestly and all the rest. Isn't that really what's important about being a Christian?"

"And I commend you for it," Ted rejoined, "but none of that makes you a Christian, at least not in the sense in which that term was used by the first Christians."

"And how did they use it?"

"Very carefully!" said Ted. "They used it to refer to a follower of Jesus Christ. More precisely, it meant one who believed what Jesus taught and did what he said. That's what I mean when I call myself a Christian. But what gave you the clue that I might be *religious,* as you say?"

"The cross, for one thing," Graham replied, pointing to Ted's lapel.

"That's it?" Ted was incredulous. "That's not much to go on for such a sweeping claim."

"Well . . ." Graham paused, peering at Ted out of the corner of his eyes, wondering what his reaction might be to his next statement. "There was one other thing."

"I can't wait to hear it."

"Weren't you just saying something about morality or right and wrong? I didn't quite get it."

"Yes. I was saying you had a moral right to hold any view

you wanted on the issue of the existence of God. Of course that raises the question whether there is any such thing as real right and wrong at all. You know, the kind that doesn't depend on how anyone might feel or think about the matter."

"Well, there you go. Who else but a religious type, or a 'Christian' as you prefer to be called, would be interested in a question like that?"

"As a matter of fact," Ted replied, "a lot of people—like you, for instance."

"I'm afraid I've got you there. Remember, I'm an atheist."

"You keep saying that. But didn't you just tell me what a decent, moral person you are? You know, paying the bills, honesty and fairness? You obviously assumed these are good things. I mean really good. What's more, you expected me and everyone else automatically to agree with you about that."

"Boy, this should be fun!" Graham shook his head. "What are you, a lawyer?"

"No, a professor. I work with ideas. It's my job and I enjoy it."

"I can see that. I'll have to watch my words more carefully around you. Okay, so I do have some interest in morality. What's it to you?"

"I'll get to that, but look, here comes the fellow who's been standing in the corner watching us."

As Graham turned to look, a tall man whose silver hair was perfectly in place drew closer. His well-pressed suit was a fitting match for the lavish surroundings, Graham thought.

"My name's Ted," said Ted, extending his hand.

"William," the other man responded in a resonating baritone voice and a distinct British accent. *Oxford,* Ted thought, but didn't ask.

"Well, William," said Ted, extending his hand, "may we ask what brings you here?"

"I don't know," replied William, as he removed his gold-framed glasses. "I just received this . . ."

"Not another unsigned invitation?" interrupted Ted. "I suppose it looked something like this?"

William chortled. "That's the one. I take it you two don't know why you're here either."

"Haven't a clue," they replied in unison.

"As I said," added Ted, "someone's up to something."

All was silent for a moment as they gazed around at their delightful surroundings.

Suddenly Graham broke the silence. "Can you believe the company I'm keeping? First I get chauffeured to this huge place, then I meet a professor who loves ideas, then a British bloke." Turning to William, he said, "I've just met Ted here, and I can already tell you he is an enigma." *Introducing evolution and secular humanism*

"And why would you say that?" inquired William.

Graham laughed. "A professor who loves ideas and arguments, and a Christian at that. If that isn't a surprising combination."

"But you didn't mention . . ." William stopped abruptly.

"That I am a Christian?" Ted cut in.

"Yes. Well, then, since we're announcing our worldviews, I might as well tell you I'm an evolutionist. The origins of the world have always been a personal interest of mine. In fact, I'm here on a six-month Royal Research Grant funded by my government. I imagine we could have some good debates!"

Graham and Ted shook their heads and stared at one another. Before either could speak, Ted noticed another man across the room signaling for their attention. "Do we know that man?" he asked.

The Englishman laughed and waved the other man over. "He and I met just moments ago. You won't believe what he's carrying in his pocket. Show them, Ian."

And with that the new guest pulled out another invitation.

"You're not going to tell us that's anonymous," sighed Ted.

"I am unless you can find a signature on it," he said, letting out a wheezy smoker's cough that was as distracting as it was unpleasant. He was a nervous, short man with heavy eyebrows and a swarthy complexion.

"So you don't know why you're here either," exclaimed Ted.

"No, I don't, but what brings you gentlemen here?"

"We don't know!" they replied in unison.

"By the way," said the new guest, extending his hand, "my name is Ian. So who have we here?"

"We have," said William, "me, William, the evolutionist, Graham the atheist and Ted the Christian. Whoever heard of such a combination? By the way, Ted here is also a professor who has a way with words and ideas. You're going to want to choose yours carefully around him."

At that Ian let out a roar of laughter. "I've just returned from the monthly meeting of our local Humanist Society."

"A humanist, eh?"

"That's right, and I can see there is going to be limited agreement with my views here."

"Your views being . . . ?" pressed Ted.

"For starters, that man is the measure of all things, by which we mean humankind, of course."

"You mean man is king?"

"I mean humans have greater dignity and value than anything else in existence. And when it comes to morals, humans are also the ground and basis of all morality."[1]

"Morality!" exclaimed Graham. "That's what Ted was talking about a moment ago. He was trying to tell us that everyone has an interest in it."

"I'd agree with that," responded Ian. "At least we humanists are concerned about it."

"There you go, Graham," added Ted.

"But," continued Ian, "I can't imagine what agreement Ted and I would have beyond that. You see, we humanists don't look beyond ourselves for the basis of morality. That's why we're called 'humanists.' We leave the supernatural to others, if there is such a thing."

"As I said," interjected Graham, "this should be fun."

Turning to Ian, Ted said, "Actually we would probably

agree on more than you think. But for now is it safe to say that you are assuming that human nature can provide an adequate basis for real right and wrong?"

"Absolutely. Of course, I suppose you Christians would think otherwise. But let's be rational about it. What reason can there be for having to look beyond humans?"

"Now that is what we'll have to find out."

At that moment, the fifth person, a young, well-dressed woman across the room, placed a book back on a shelf and turned toward the others. Her dark brown hair was cut in a short, contemporary style, and as she walked it swung back to reveal a pair of sparkling earrings.

Ethical relativism

"Excuse me, gentlemen," she said, removing her designer glasses. "I couldn't help overhearing. You were saying something about morality?" Her ready smile showed off glacier-white teeth.

"We were," replied Graham. "Our friend Ted here was asking whether any of us thought—how did you put it, Ted?—that there was any real right and wrong."

Ted nodded. "I was speaking of objective right and wrong. The kind that does not depend on what anyone thinks or feels about it."

"What luck!" exclaimed the young woman. "I'm a graduate student. Francine is my name. This is a topic of great interest to me. Of course, being a moral relativist I approach moral questions quite differently from the way some others do."

"A moral relativist, are you, Francine?" said Ted.

"Yes, I'm in the process of writing my master's thesis right now. I'm arguing for moral relativism."

"In other words, Francine, you believe there is no such thing as real, objective right and wrong."

"That's me. It all depends upon the person and situation. In fact, statements of right and wrong are really only expressions of someone's emotions or attitude toward an action."[2]

"So what is wrong for one person may well be right for another?"

Truth: not time
dependent

"Exactly. And why not? One person's attitude or feelings about some action may be different from someone else's. And why should we burden ourselves with outdated ideas about moral rules anyway? Circumstances change, and our moral ideas should change with them."

"Are you saying we should evaluate ideas by looking at the clock?"

"What! Who said anything about a clock?"

"You did," said Ted. "You just said that an idea should be rejected because it's old, outdated."

"Well, maybe there's more to it than that."

"There certainly is. When I want to disprove an idea, I've got to show that it is *false*. Your argument against objective moral standards was simply that they are outdated. That is a clock word, or calendar word. After all, calendars are only long clocks. And surely you're not going to tell us that everything said by Plato or Aristotle or George Washington or Sojourner Truth or Winston Churchill is false simply because it's old?"[3]

"Okay, I get your point," said Francine. "But who am I or you or anyone else to impose our moral sentiments on others?"[4]

"Of course," replied Ted, "the important question still is whether your understanding of morals is true. Let's face it. Regardless of how tolerant you may be, if your view is wrong, we would still be mistaken to believe it."

"Good point," Graham cut in. "I say we should discuss it further." Then, turning to the young woman, he said, "I should have warned you, our professor here has a way of catching one in her own words. So be careful!"

"By the way," said Ted to Francine, "dare I ask what brings you here? No. Let me guess. You received an unsigned invitation, and here you are."

"But how did you know?"

"Because we all have them. The same as yours."

"So why are we here?" she asked.

"We don't know," answered Graham, "but what a crowd!"

"Shall we?" said Ted, motioning at the table. Along with many kinds of fruit, there were pastries, rolls, cheeses, pickles and sandwich meats, all provided by the mystery host. After they filled their plates, they moved toward the chairs.

Francine settled back into a recliner and took a bite of a pastry. "Not only is this room comfortable," she said, "but this food tastes so good it must be sinful."

"Now that," cut in Ted, "assumes there is such a thing as sin—or shall we say right and wrong. Weren't you the one who said things like that didn't exist?"

Francine shook her head, whistling ever so softly. "I can see I'm going to have to watch my words around here."

"What did I tell you?" Graham chuckled.

"Well, now that we're on the topic," continued Ted, sounding more like a professor all the time, "what do you all think? Is there any real right and wrong?" *Defining objective morality*

The abruptness of the question caught them slightly off guard, so he went on. "Are there any actions, attitudes, characteristics or the like which can properly be called morally right or wrong—I mean, for all people, regardless of how anyone might feel about the matter?"

"Well, you all know my answer to that," said Francine confidently. "Real right and wrong is an illusion. It doesn't exist. It's sheer intolerance to think we somehow have a lock on moral truth so we can impose it on others. Nor is there any good reason to think such a thing exists in the first place."

"That's very fashionable, and I'm sure it's good philosophical fun," responded William with a smile, "but surely we have to call certain things really right and wrong."

"But that's arrogance! It's playing God!" argued Francine.

"Hey!" yelled Graham. "Before I have to decide on this question, I want to make sure I understand it. What would it mean for there to be no real moral right or wrong?"

"Fair enough," agreed Ted. "A good first step. Let's clarify our question. Of course, there are only two possible answers. Either there *is* this kind of real right and wrong or there

isn't. And as you can well imagine, both of these answers
have their proponents. Those who answer no to our question believe all morality to be a strictly *subjective* affair. Those
who disagree believe it to be *objective.*"

"Meaning?" said Graham.

"Yes, yes," said Ted with an approving nod. "Those terms
subjective and *objective.*"

"Let me handle this part," spoke up Francine. "After all,
I'm the ethical relativist here."

"Be my guest."

Defining   "If we were to call moral judgments *subjective,*" she said,
subjective "wouldn't that mean we thought they were like the things
morality   we say about the way things taste?"

"Well put," Ted answered, "but go on."

"Well, for instance," she continued, "it just so happens
that I quite enjoy lobster, especially when served with a nice
cut of T-bone steak. Now if I were to say, 'Lobster tastes
good,' my statement would be true."

They all agreed.

"But," she added, "it would also be subjective, because its
truth would depend entirely on the attitude or belief of the
speaking subject—in this case, me. Because I like lobster,
for me to say it tastes good is a true statement."

"Hmm," mused Graham.

"Now, on the other hand," she said, looking directly at
him, "*you* may wonder how anyone could possibly endure
the taste of a lobster."

"You're right on that score."

"You then might taste the same lobster and pronounce it
unfit for human consumption. Or, to put it more technically,
you might say, 'Lobster tastes awful.' "

"Your point being?" said Graham.

"That because you do not enjoy the taste of lobster, your
statement would also be correct."

"Yes!" said Ted. "That is exactly the point. Two subjective
statements can conflict with each other and still both be
correct. Their truth depends entirely on the attitude, opin-

ion or belief of the speaking subjects."

Graham leaned back in his chair, carefully contemplating Francine's illustration. "This would mean, then," he said, "that there could be no such thing as a subjective statement that is false. I mean, how could there be?"

"Very perceptive," said Francine. "And you are almost right."

"Almost?" asked Graham, somewhat impatiently.

"That's what I said. You see, subjective statements will be true so long as one simple condition is met."

"Which is?"

"I think we said it just a moment ago," she said with a twinkle. "Didn't we just say that because you do not enjoy the taste of lobster, your statement that you do not would be correct?"

Graham nodded.

"Well, there you have it," said Francine, leaning back into her chair. "If subjectively true statements are true because they reflect the attitude or belief of the one making them, then it will follow that they will be true only so long as they do, in fact, accurately represent the speaker's attitude."

"In other words," responded Graham, "if I do not like lobster but for some reason say I *do,* my statement becomes false."

"Precisely," cut in Ted. "Which all goes to show that subjective statements are not really statements of fact about the item spoken of in any ordinary sense. Neither your statement about lobster nor Francine's really tells us anything about lobsters. If you reported to us that they are edible sea crustaceans with compound eyes, long antennae and five pairs of legs, and that after eating them some people say they like the flavor and others don't, it *would* tell us something about the lobsters themselves. Instead, your statements tell us something about *you.* They tell us that you do or do not like the taste of these creatures, nothing more."

Francine nodded, even though she had to admit she had never thought about this implication of her relativism.

"But," said Ted, glancing at his watch, "let's get to your question. What would it mean then to say that all moral judgments are strictly subjective?"

"I assume," said Graham, "that it would mean they would be exactly like those judgments of personal taste. Moral judgments will never be false so long as the one making them believes them."

"Correct! And here is where it becomes interesting. This will be true even if two of us make conflicting moral judgments about the same act!"

At that point Graham lapsed into an introspective state, his lips moving as though in a trance. "Just like the lobsters," he said, after some time.

"Yes, like the lobsters! If, that is, one is persuaded that morality is strictly a subjective matter.[5]

Objective morality: real right and wrong

"But we said at the beginning of our discussion that there were two possible answers to this question about the true nature of moral statements," Ted reminded them.

"Right," said Graham. "There are also those who believe morality is an *objective* commodity. I take it that on this view, moral judgments are not at all like our judgments of personal taste."

"And you're right," answered Ted. "But what *are* they like?"

Graham took a moment to collect his thoughts. "Why, of course. They would be considered true or false regardless of how anyone believed or felt about the matter."

"He's on the mark," said Ted to the others. And then leaning toward them, he spoke softly. "Follow me carefully here, because we must get a clear idea of the meaning of this term *objective*. You see, if a statement is objective, it means its truth does *not* depend upon the attitude or opinion of the speaking subject."

"You mean the person making the statement," said Graham.

"Right. Look at it this way. When we speak of objective truth, we are dealing with truth that, we might say, is out there. It is beyond any of us. It is not determined or controlled by us. All we do is recognize it."

The discussion lulled as Ian distributed coffee and sweets. After the sugar and cream were sorted out and they had started sipping, Graham spoke up. "So if I were to say that there were five of us in the room here today, as we speak, that statement would be true."

"Profound," smirked Francine.

"But," said Graham, his voice rising, "it is also *objectively* true, because the fact that it is true does not depend on what I or any other person believe about the number of people in this room."

"Precisely!" responded Ted, rising from his chair. "It would be true even if none of us believed it or even knew of it, for that matter. So then let's humor ourselves and imagine someone were to join us right now and disagree with us on this matter. Suppose she were to declare that there are nine or ten of us present. How might we respond to this disagreeable person?"

"Well," said Graham wryly, "we could say, 'It's a free country, go ahead and disagree.' "

"Clever," remarked Francine.

"We could even defend this disagreeable person's right to disagree."

"Aren't we magnanimous tonight?" responded Ted. "But the one response we could never give our new guest is . . ."

"We could never tell her she was correct," Graham interrupted.

"Absolutely," declared Ted. "She just happens to be plain wrong on this point. That is because the fact that, including her, there are now six of us in the room is *objectively* true, and there's not much we can do to change that. Objective truth is a very stubborn thing. But back to our main question again. What would it mean for moral judgments to be objective?"

"Now it's clear," answered Graham. "If a moral judgment is objectively true, it is true regardless of how anyone thinks or feels about the matter. If someone disagrees, we may respond as kindly as we wish, but we cannot tell them they are correct."

"Well said," responded Ted. "If morality is objective, then we are dealing with something—let's call it moral truth or moral value—that is out there, beyond any individual person. This moral value is not determined by us. We merely recognize it, and it doesn't matter how anyone feels about it. It is what it is, and that's that.[6]

"Well, there you have it," he continued. "Objective versus subjective morality. A very important issue indeed. But let us be clear about one thing. So far we have said nothing about which of these two answers is correct. That will have to come later, but at least we now know what they mean."

They were so engrossed in discussion that they didn't even notice the reserved man at the door. He was trying to get their attention. "Uh, excuse me," he said softly, but to no avail. "Excuse me!" he repeated sharply.

The others jumped and turned to him.

"Sorry to disturb you, but it's 2:00 p.m. and your rides are waiting."

"Can you believe that?" exclaimed Francine. "It's time to go. Let's meet again."

"You are all invited for lunch again at the same time next week," interrupted the reserved man.

The setting, the food and lively discussion had dispelled any apprehension. After exchanging business cards, they all readily accepted his invitation.

2
WHAT IF MORALITY WERE SUBJECTIVE?
The Consequences of Subjective Morality

T ed glanced at the calendar again. Sure enough, it was the sixteenth already. Periodically, over the week, his mind had been taken up with thoughts of last week's discussion. At exactly 11:30 a.m. he heard the sound of a car out front. He knew his ride had arrived. Whoever this mystery host was, he or she obviously valued precision.

As the limousine made its way across town, Ted suspected the discussion of last week was only the beginning. It had raised more questions than it had answered. But one thing he was convinced of was that this meeting of the minds didn't just happen. It was no coincidence. Someone or something was behind it, and he hoped that someday he would find out who.

The same man was at the door again, and Ted grasped

his hand. "Ted's my name, but I didn't catch yours."

"I'm . . . I'm . . . Well, maybe you should just think of me as the doorkeeper." By this time they were at the same reception room. The lavish surroundings were as impressive as before. Familiarity had not dulled appreciation.

Ted's four counterparts were already actively engaging one another. After helping himself to a drink from the table prepared for them, Ted joined them, and Graham turned toward him. "Hi, Ted. We're already beyond the small talk and into the interesting stuff.

"As I recall," he continued, "last week we were clarifying our question, asking what it would mean for morality to be either objective or subjective."

"So we were," responded Francine, "and what a journey that took us on."

"Ah, but that was only a start," interrupted Ted.

"Somehow I guessed that."

"In fact," continued Ted, "I would even go so far as to say that no sooner do we get that question clarified than we are faced with an even more significant one."

Their suspicions were confirmed. But what their professor friend had in mind was not clear. Then, slipping into his oft-used Socratic style, Ted asked, "Where do you think we ought to go from here? Once the meaning of the question has been made clear, what is our next step?"

"Why, our next inquiry must be into which of these two views on morality is the more correct!" exclaimed William. "We talked about that last week. Which should we believe if we want to know the truth?"

"That's it!" echoed Ian. "Now that we know precisely what the question means, why not try to answer it?"

"Indeed," responded Ted, "you're both on the right track." Then, leaning forward, he removed his eyeglasses and gestured with them as if to signify the importance of his next few words. He said in low tones, "We do need to get there, but that task must wait for the right moment. If we were to tackle it now, we would be skipping a most important idea, a transitional step actually. We would be missing an idea that will relate both to our previous task of clarifying our question and also to that future step you both just mentioned of determining which of our two answers is superior."

Ian admitted that if there were such a step, they shouldn't miss it. But he said he couldn't imagine what it might be.

Ted laughed cheerfully. Then, getting up, he went to the large array of plants organized by the west window and, with a gardener's eye, appreciated the well-kept greenery. The others glanced at each other and waited a moment.

Inescapable consequences of our viewpoints

"Well?" said Graham, more than a little impatiently. "This step?"

Turning to them, still smiling, Ted asked whether they thought consequences of ideas were important.

"I don't follow," stammered Francine.

"Well," continued Ted, "isn't it true that no idea stands in isolation as an island unto itself? Don't ideas form networks with each idea, having relationships with other ideas?"

"I assume there is a point to all of this?" Francine asked.

"Hmmm. Ideas having relations," Graham mused with a smile, his voice barely audible. The very thought struck him as humorous. "Never thought of it that way before."

"But it's true," replied Ted. "Some ideas are related to other ideas as assumptions or presuppositions standing behind them. Isn't that how the notion of human free will relates to the notion of human responsibility? When we hold a person responsible for his actions, whether good or bad, aren't we assuming he performed them freely? Aren't we saying to him, 'You could have done otherwise but didn't'? When we fine a motorist for a traffic violation, we are assuming the motorist did not have to violate the law. She did so freely. You see, our idea that a person is free to do other than she did stands behind our idea that she is responsible for her actions."

Some ideas presuppose others

"Seems correct to me," said William.

Some ideas are the consequences of others

"And," continued Ted, "some ideas are related to other ideas as their consequences. For instance, if I accept the idea that only a fool would believe the earth was flat, then, upon learning that my neighbor believes the earth is flat, I am obliged also to accept the idea that my neighbor is a fool. My acceptance of the first idea entails my acceptance of the second, because it is a consequence of the first. I cannot hold the first without the second, nor can I reject the second without also rejecting the first.

Some ideas are incompatible with other ideas

"There are still other relations between ideas. Some are incompatible with others; that is, believing one entails rejecting the other. For instance, the ideas that my friend Tom is a Marxist and that he is a capitalist are incompatible with each other. They cannot both be true."

Then, pausing, Ted added, "But we need not press this line of thought any further for the time being."[1]

"Yes," objected Francine. "What is the importance of all of this?"

"I think I may see where you're heading," said Graham, leaning forward. "If all ideas are related to other ideas, then anytime we accept an idea as true, we have—like it or not— accepted other ideas as well."

"Uh-huh."

"And, for that matter, we've rejected still others—namely, all those that are incompatible with the one we accepted."

"You've read my mind!" exclaimed Ted.

Inescapable consequences of our moral views

"But what does that have to do with our question whether morality is objective or subjective?" Francine persisted.

"It has everything to do with it. Can't you see?" exclaimed Graham. "It also applies to these two ideas. Once we accept the idea that morality is objective or subjective, we will have to live with certain other ideas whether we like them or not."

"Right," agreed Ted. "And it doesn't matter how much we like or dislike a particular idea, how appealing it may be or how unbearable, for that matter." His arms chopped the air to help make his point. "Once we decide morality is either subjective or objective, we will also have to accept certain other ideas. They are just part of the network—the uninvited guests, if you will."

They all laughed at his analogy but knew it to be true.

"The point being . . . ?" queried Francine.

"That we will be wise to investigate the consequences of either of these two answers *before* we commit ourselves to them rather than after."

"I see," responded Francine. "And that's why you referred to this step as a transitional step."

"Exactly! It is still part clarification, but it also moves us toward reasons for accepting one or the other of the two answers."

The conversation lulled as they shifted positions and let this transitional step sink in.

In a moment, Ted spoke again. "There is one thing we need to be clear on when it comes to the consequences of any viewpoint. We mentioned a moment ago that a knowledge of the consequences of ideas moves us toward *reasons* for accepting or rejecting those ideas."

The others nodded.

"This is where extreme caution is needed," he added. "You see, we are tempted to think that if a particular viewpoint has bad consequences, then the viewpoint must be mistaken."

Graham became pensive. "Well, isn't it?" he queried.

Ted leaned forward in his chair, glasses in hand, and said quite intensely, "Follow me carefully here, because I may have to contradict an idea that is widely accepted."

"Something you obviously enjoy doing," Graham quipped.

"It's that obvious, is it? Well, it's true that there are actually two kinds of bad consequences any viewpoint or idea could have. Some consequences are bad in the sense that they are *unappealing* and we don't like them, but that is all that is bad about them. Haven't you heard people say, 'I don't believe in God because I couldn't stand the thought of having someone putting limits on me or telling me what I can and can't

Distinguishing two kinds of bad consequences

Some are merely unappealing

do'? But of course, if it turns out that God's existence entails certain unappealing implications, that doesn't mean he does not exist. In fact, it has nothing to do with the issue of God's existence. God still may exist, and if he does, certain consequences will follow and that's that."

"In other words," responded Francine, wanting to articulate the idea for herself, "unappealing consequences of any idea do not mean the idea is false."

"Exactly."

"But doesn't it also work the other way around?" Graham shot back. "An appealing consequence of an idea does not mean the idea is correct either."

"Equally true," remarked Ted.

"So to believe in God because it produces a wonderful sense of security is also fallacious."

"You atheists don't miss a beat, do you?"

"Just wanting to be complete."

"Well, you're right. This attractive consequence doesn't mean God exists any more than the unattractive consequence meant he didn't. It simply is not a reason to believe one way or the other about that important question."

"Okay, we've got it," said Francine.

Some bad consequences are impossible

"But if you'll recall," Ted continued, "I said there is another kind of bad consequence. This other kind *can* constitute an argument against the idea that produces it. It can actually disprove it. Any suggestions?" he asked with a look of intrigue.

Here was the professor in action, living out his conviction that if people came up with the idea on their own, not only would they learn it much better but they would also develop their intellectual skills. The others stared at each other.

Ted rose from his chair momentarily to stretch his legs. "Any takers?" he asked again.

"Well, for starters," said Francine, not quite sure of where she was going, "if the bad consequences of a viewpoint can actually show that view to be wrong, then there must be something more wrong with them than just that they are unappealing."

"So far so good," said Ted. "So then, what must be wrong with them?"

Until this time Graham had been following quietly. Suddenly, bolting upright in his chair, he exclaimed, "What if the view had a consequence that we *knew* could not be true?"

"That's it!" Ted waved his hands, almost spilling his drink in his enthusiasm. "A viewpoint that produces an absurd or impossible consequence is, itself, thereby reduced to an absurdity."

"You've lost me," complained Francine.

"Actually, you are much more familiar with this technique than you realize," Ted said, smiling.

Francine said she doubted that.

Ted, undaunted, continued, "You are familiar with the theory called hard determinism, aren't you? It asserts that human beings are not free, that our actions are determined by some external causes. They could not be other than they are."

Francine said she was.

"Well," continued Ted, "some use this strategy to argue against that theory. They argue that if hard determinism were true, then human responsibility for our actions would cease to exist. But since we are convinced we are responsible for our actions, we must also believe that hard determinism is false."[2]

"Francine, don't you see?" spoke up Graham. "Because hard determinism forces us to believe another idea that we believe isn't true, it too must be false." Turning to Ted, he asked, "Aren't we doing the same thing when we make lighthearted statements like 'If you're a conservative, then I'm Roger Rabbit'? I mean, isn't that simply our way of denying that someone is a conservative, to show that it implies an obviously absurd idea?"

"Ah," said Ted, with an affirming grin, "making up your own examples. A clear sign that you've got it."

"I suggest we refill our cups," piped up Ian.

"Agreed!" exclaimed Ted.

With that, they all made their way to the table and began filling their plates from the cold cuts and salads set out.

Moral action and the nature of morality   Francine took a drink and a plate of food and wandered over to one of the large windows overlooking the estate. As she took in the beauty of the grounds and garden, her thoughts returned to the discussion. She knew this was no ordinary conversation. It wasn't that she was not enjoying it; she was, greatly. It was that she knew there could be profound consequences to it all. This was no mere academic chat. Furthermore, it dealt directly with the moral relativism that was so important to her.

It was no secret that she had always prided herself on being a self-described "moral person." She usually did the right thing. What was more, she was quick to speak out against immoral practices when she saw them. Last year the university newspaper ran an article with racist overtones. Francine fired off an angry response. And she had personally led the fight with the administration for new, stringent regulations against sexual harassment of students.

She had always looked with a certain disdain upon people who didn't seem to care about these things. They were morally inferior, though she shied away from using that term.

But she could now see that all these ideas she held so strongly depended on certain views about morality. She became uneasy as she wondered what her ideas would mean if she dared apply them consistently.

Suddenly her thoughts were interrupted by the sound of Ted's voice. "Beautiful, isn't it?"

"What's that? Oh, yes, the grounds."

Ted laughed. "I can see you were deep in thought."

"Perceptive, aren't you?"

"Well, some things are obvious."

"It's just that I couldn't help but wonder where all of this is taking us. I mean, these thoughts that we're bouncing around so freely may have serious implications for the way we had better respond to moral issues."

"I see," mused Ted, "and those potential consequences are causing you some concern."

She nodded.

Pausing for just a moment, he asked, "Which consequences most concern you?"

"That's the whole problem," Francine said, her voice rising. "I don't know! But I know they're out there whether I know them or not. That became pretty clear in there." She pointed to the room they had just come from.

"I see, I see."

"And it's also clear," she continued, "that the consequences will likely be serious. If we decide morality is objective, there will be consequences. If we decide it is subjective, again there will be consequences. My problem is that I don't know what they are."

"It's true!" exclaimed Ted. "Ideas do have consequences. In fact, I think I should warn you that some of the consequences we're talking about may surprise you, even shock you. But as we said before, they are the uninvited guests of any idea. They don't go away simply because we don't like them. So we might as well know about them."

For a moment neither one spoke. They both stared out the window, sipping their drinks, with only the soft hum of the other conversations in the background.

Suddenly Ted noticed the time. "It's 2:00!" he exclaimed. "My ride will be here any minute now!"

"Hey! Hey! What about those consequences?" Francine asked. "Aren't we going to explore them? Even a hint, a clue?"

"Funny you'd ask," Ted answered. "Yes, we will examine them, but I'm afraid it's too early to let that cat out of the bag just yet."

Then it was Francine's turn to laugh.

"Are you aware of the special lectures we're holding on campus next week?" he continued.

"I've seen the posters."

"Well, I'm slated to give the talk on this very topic next Tuesday. I hope you'll be there."

Just then the doorkeeper walked in and announced that they were all invited once again for a light lunch on the day following the lecture.

Ted was surprised. "You knew about . . ."

"The lecture?" responded the doorkeeper. "Why, yes, of course."

"But how?"

The doorkeeper raised his eyebrows but said nothing. Ted shook his head but then recalled the advertising and realized that this quiet man must be more current than he had thought. Who *was* he? And the mystery host. Where was he? What else did he know? Whoever he was, he had certainly been successful in bringing this group together. By this time the group felt a sense of camaraderie. They were becoming not just participants in a discussion but associates in the search for truth. And they were enjoying it. The impressive surroundings only added to the pleasure. All enthusiastically agreed to meet again.

As Ted turned to leave, he stopped and looked back at Francine. "About those consequences," he called out. "You asked for a hint."

"Yes!"

"Here's a preview. You ignore consequences at your peril!"

"That's it?" she called back.

"Isn't that enough? See you Tuesday!"

As Francine sat alone, she realized she was getting in deeper. But then again, how perilous could consequences be? As she jotted down Ted's lecture on her calendar, she remembered that consequences could actually make or break a viewpoint. Anything that powerful was worth looking into.

3
SUBJECTIVE MORALITY FOUND WANTING
The Case Against Subjective Morality

T ed surveyed the auditorium from his seat on the platform. He would have preferred the more casual setting of a classroom, but the amount of interest shown in this topic precluded that.

To his left he noticed Francine and Graham coming in with a group of friends. He was glad they were there and quickly asked a colleague standing nearby to meet them.

"I'd like to introduce two recent acquaintances who challenge my thinking," he said. "Francine and Graham."

"You're here to scrutinize Ted's every argument, are you?" joked the colleague.

"Just part of an ongoing discussion," responded Graham.

"Don't let these two fool you with their modesty," Ted advised. "Francine here is a graduate student specializing in moral relativism, and Graham is president of SPAR."

"SPAR? I should know what that is," the colleague wondered aloud.

"The Society for the Promotion of Atheistic Research," responded Graham.

"Yes, yes. I've heard of your organization. So you're the president?"

"That's right. Which is why it's especially important to hear a Christian theist lecture on morality."

"A view from the far side," chuckled the colleague. "But I guess we'd all better find a seat while there are still a few left."

Assumptions in our ordinary conversation   It wasn't as if the two young skeptics didn't have other things to do. They did. But since the luncheons they had been doing a lot of thinking about which of the two views of morality was correct.

In their common everyday moral statements, they were already assuming one or the other. Being a moral relativist, Francine was assuming a purely subjective foundation for all moral judgments. But she had to admit she had never considered what consequences might follow from her stand.

What tolerance means for morality   Graham, on the other hand, did not accept that all moral value was purely subjective. He realized full well that, on one level, that view had a certain appeal to many people, including some atheists like himself. It appeared so tolerant, so fashionable, so open-minded toward others' views. These were qualities he admired. In fact, he looked with disgust on certain groups in society which tried to force their narrow agendas on others. He knew that if we are all to get along with each other in this world, we must tolerate others' different views.

Yet on another level there was something unacceptable about the notion that all morality is determined by individual attitudes or emotions. Surely some actions had to be wrong, really wrong, regardless of how the person doing them felt.

As Ted looked out, he could see that the front half of the

auditorium was filled with university students while the back included people from the surrounding community. The master of ceremonies was completing his introduction while a few stragglers were coming in. A man slipped into the last row. Had Ted noticed, he might have recognized him as the doorkeeper.

People were settling themselves, and Ted was ready. "And now, without further delay," he heard the emcee say, "would you join me in welcoming Professor Theo Douglas." There was a smattering of applause as he nodded to Ted and then found his way to a seat.

Ted stepped to the podium, placed his notes before him and began: "Let me commend you for taking an evening to listen to a lecture on this topic." Then he joked, "Even though I am the speaker, I have to tell you that I don't really enjoy listening to speakers. In fact, I imagine that if I were in your shoes I wouldn't be here. So we'll try to make this as painless as possible." Light laughter spread through the room.

"I should say at the outset, however, that we are quite lucky this evening. We won't have to work very hard at making this topic relevant. In fact, few topics could be more relevant to the way you and I live than ours today. That is because of the sheer number of moral judgments we all make. They fill our daily conversation.

"I would be willing to bet," he continued, "that many of us have made at least one such statement since entering this auditorium tonight. In fact, how many of you, since coming into this room, have called some action, characteristic or attitude good or bad? Or you've said something ought or ought not to be? It could have been something your spouse or neighbor did, or the government enacted, or something you overheard. I'm talking about any kind of moral value judgment."

The frequency of our moral judgments

There was a collective chuckle throughout the room as hands timidly began to rise.

"Let me be clear," continued Ted, "that we have no reason

to be ashamed or embarrassed about such statements. They are a legitimate part of normal human conversation. A sense of morality is one thing that sets us apart from the animal world.

"But let's ask another question. This is only for those of you who raised your hands. How many of you are aware that when you made your moral judgment, you were assuming something very fundamental about morality as a whole? You were assuming it is either an objective commodity or a subjective one." This time there were fewer hands.

"Well, you were," he continued, "and that leads me to the question of the evening. Tonight we are asking, Is morality subjective or is it objective? Some of you may have questions as we go. Please make a note of them. We'll take time at the end for at least a few.

"Now I must say at the outset that I will be assuming a few things tonight. First, I will assume we all know the meaning of our two key terms, *objective* and *subjective*. The ushers have distributed handouts with brief explanations of these terms for your review, if needed.

"Second, I will assume we all have a working knowledge of what is meant by the terms *objective morality* and *subjective morality*. I know that many of you do understand them, because our lecturer last week used them in his argument.[1]

Subjective morality's first problem: its consequences

"Now it seems," he went on, "that there is widespread— if not universal—agreement on the notion that morality is objective, that it is not subjective."

He paused for a moment to let the import of that sentence sink in. "Let me clarify," he added. "I do not mean to say that no one argues that morality is subjective. As a matter of fact, some do. What I mean is that virtually all of us, if we were to ponder for just a short while what a world without objective morality would be like, would agree that morality is an objective commodity."

At that comment, people around the room stopped writing and looked up quizzically. *The power of consequences,* Francine thought to herself, recalling their last talk. She wondered how convincing Ted would be.

"I think this is best seen," Ted continued, "by simply taking note of what it would mean for all morality to be subjective.

"Let's imagine, for purposes of argument, that morality really were a strictly subjective commodity. What would follow from this? Well, first of all, this would mean that the moral statements we all make would be exactly like our judgments about the way things taste. There would be no question of their being right or wrong. Their truth, or shall we say correctness, would depend strictly upon the attitude, opinion or belief of the person making them. He or she is the individual subject.

"We already agreed that a person could never be called wrong for uttering the words 'Spinach is good.' That is because the truth or falsity of that statement depends entirely upon the attitude or opinion of the person making it. We call that person the speaking subject. If he likes it, to him it is good. I cannot call his statement wrong even if I don't like it—which I don't!" he added with zest.

"Now here is the point, for our purposes. If morality is subjective, then moral statements will be just like all the things we say about the way things taste. That will mean, of course, that your and my moral judgments could conflict and still both be correct.

"But there's more," he continued. "If morality were entirely subjective, then our moral judgments about certain actions or things would not really be saying anything about those actions or things at all. Rather, they would only be saying something about us, the speakers. When I say, 'Liver is awful,' I'm not really saying anything about liver at all, am I? I'm saying something about myself. I am telling you that I don't like it. In the same way, assuming morality is subjective, if I were to say a particular action is wrong, all I would really be saying is 'I don't like that action' or 'That action offends me.' My attitude toward that action would be revealed, but that's all. You see, that's what we mean by

Subjective moral judgments: a matter of taste

Subjective moral judgments: one-person specific

calling a statement subjective. Its truth or falsity hinges upon the speaking subject."

He paused to let the note-takers get that thought down. He was well aware of how new those last couple of ideas would be to some in the audience. And from the anxious looks crossing some faces, he could tell that they were also thought-provoking. But this was good. His purpose here was to stimulate thought, to provide new information and to help people think through the issue carefully. This was the only way to come closer to the truth. An example or two would help this process along, he thought.

Subjective morality applied to specific social activities "Perhaps an illustration would help," Ted went on. "Some of us have heard of the gender discrimination that has been evident in our community recently." Heads were nodding. "I dare say that some of us here today have spoken up against it.

"But you see, if morality is entirely subjective, then discriminating against a person because he or she is a member of a different race, religion or gender is not really wrong. I mean that it is not wrong in any objective sense that would be obligatory or binding on anyone else. It may offend your personal moral taste, but you'll have to recognize that others may have different moral tastes that are just as right as yours—that is, if morality is subjective.

"Let me give another example. We all know about that small circle of government officials that has been so prominent in the press recently. You know the ones."

He could see people smiling grimly at each other. "Do we!" someone shot back from the front row.

"Oh, I've touched a raw nerve, have I?" Ted went on with a laugh. "Well, if we're to believe the reports, some of them have been using their public offices for personal gain. We've all heard of the secret phone calls, the special favors allegedly given.

"If you read the editorial columns at all, you'll know what I mean when I say these officials have been denounced in the strongest of terms. As one columnist put it, 'These actions are an abuse of the public trust, a moral outrage.' Another called these officials 'morally bankrupt.'

"Now, if I had to place bets, I would say that after our next election more than a few of these people will be looking for a new line of work."

A ripple of laughter spread over the auditorium. An older man with wavy silver hair shouted from the back, "Let's hope so!"

"Ah, there you have it," replied Ted. "We even have a certain sense of moral outrage with us tonight. But here's the point for our issue. You or I or those columnists we just spoke of may not *like* politicians using their public office for personal gain. But if morality is strictly a subjective commodity, then all we can say about it us that we don't like it. We cannot condemn it more strongly than that. We certainly cannot say it is genuinely wrong and should not have been done regardless of how anyone felt about it. In other words, we cannot say it is wrong in any objective sense."

Suddenly heads turned as a chair near the front was noisily pushed back and a young man jumped to his feet to leave. "Nonsense!" he said angrily as he made his way toward the door. Some in the audience laughed nervously. Others glanced at each other and then at Ted to see what he might say. Ted was momentarily taken aback by the intensity of the outburst.

After the door shut behind the young man, a thoughtful silence prevailed for a few seconds, and then Ted commented dryly, "Well, I suppose that will be one fewer objection at the end. But I guess we'll never knew, will we, because we never had the opportunity to interact.

"But we could go on," he said. "The same is true for a person who kidnaps, abuses, dismembers a child and then leaves her to die, as I recently read of someone doing. Suppose someone does it to my friend, my relative or me. That may be abhorrent to me, but I cannot call that person's actions wrong *for them*. They simply offend my personal moral tastes. This person obviously has other tastes in morality, which he is equally entitled to call right or good. The same must be said for rape and sexual harassment. The same for Nazi atrocities.

"We could go further, but the point is the same. If morality is strictly subjective, then none of these actions is really wrong in any objective sense. They simply offend your or my personal views. We may not like them, but that is about all that can be said.

The basis for condemning any action

"Of course, the immediate question we're faced with then is what business we have condemning anyone for doing something when the only thing wrong with it is that we find it unappealing. We can say we don't like it, but we can't say there is anything more wrong with it than that."

Ted looked up from his notes. The audience had grown somber. The examples were harsh, he knew. He only wanted to ensure that no one missed the point.

"Let me sum up my comments about what subjective morality would mean for us." He was eager to complete this part of his lecture. "We could say it this way. If that is the true nature of morality, then it would mean each of us is free, morally speaking, to choose whichever moral point of view we find most appealing. The choice of whether to be a Mother Teresa or an Adolf Hitler would be roughly the same choice as whether to become a saxophone player or an organ player. You simply choose the one you find most appealing and worthwhile.

The conflict between consequences and what we know

"But let's ask a question about all of this. How many of us believe for a moment that this view of morality is true?"

Doubtful looks crossed many faces, but Ted could tell few were bold enough to commit themselves.

"What I mean is this. Isn't it true," he asked rhetorically, "that we know, even if we're not sure how we know, that certain actions, motives or what have you are wrong? I mean really wrong even for the person who disagrees.

"But let's push this a little further. What do we say to the person who tries to defend himself for cruel and vicious deeds done toward others by saying, 'Oh, I was just playing by the rules that our group has set up'? We reject such a defense out of hand.

"Isn't that exactly what happened after World War II at the Nuremberg trials for Nazi war crimes? The atrocities they committed were almost beyond belief. They defended themselves by saying they had made decisions within the framework of their own legal system and hence could not be judged by a different legal system.

"That defense was rejected then, and I think most of us here would reject it now as well. And rightly so."

The audience was still serious. Ted's material had been rather intense up to this point. As he mentally prepared for his next idea, he knew that something lighter would be a welcome break.

"Now some of you may be wondering, with all these troublesome consequences, 'Didn't he say earlier that there are some who believe morality is subjective?' Yes, I did say that. Some do take this position and argue for it. Maybe even some of you here. But if you do," he said with a twinkle, "and if you try to live out your position consistently, you just may encounter a couple of other difficulties on your way in addition to the ones we've just seen.[2] Let me point them out so you won't be surprised when they make their appearance."

There was a light rustling throughout the room as the audience shifted positions and mental gears.

"First," he continued, "you just may run into what we often call 'the problem of self-refutation' or 'self-reference.' The principle of self-reference is applied whenever we apply a principle to itself. We turn it back on itself and see whether or not it can stand the same test it applies to other things. My students will all be very familiar with this term."

Second difficulty: the problem of self-refutation

Some knowing chuckles filtered through the room. Certainly they knew. It was common knowledge that you couldn't take any class on any subject from Professor Douglas without hearing about the problem of self-refutation.

Somehow he found a way to apply this principle to some issue regardless of what class he was teaching.

"What I mean," Ted said, "is this. Notice what you do when you assert that morality is subjective. With this assertion you affirm that there are no objective moral principles that are binding on anyone else. Now here's the problem. It is immensely difficult to deny the existence of all objective moral principles without at the same time affirming at least one."

Eyebrows rose throughout the auditorium.

"Which is," he added, "that because there are no objective moral principles, you ought not to evaluate my actions by any such principles."

A group of students to his left laughed audibly.

"The problem with that statement is," he went on, "that it refutes itself. It is something like the statement 'I can't speak a word of English.' By speaking the sentence, I refute it. The subjectivist appears to do this same thing when she tells others they ought not to judge her by any objective moral standards. Does she really believe all moral judgments are subjective or not? She *claims* she believes this, but at the same time she implies one *objective* moral principle, which is that no one ought to judge her by any objective moral principle."

At this many in the audience nodded and smiled as they caught the point. Even if you didn't agree, you had to admit that Ted's tactic was interesting and fun.

A response to the problem of self-refutation

Suddenly a hand shot up near the back. A bookish-looking young man with wire-rimmed glasses shouted out, "But we subjectivists are not saying you *ought* not to judge our actions by any objectively binding moral principles!"

"You're not?" Ted responded.

Two kinds of judgments: rational versus moral

"No!" the young man shouted again. Others near him nodded their agreement. "We're only saying you have no basis for doing so, no rational grounds. It doesn't make sense for you to condemn my actions as objectively bad or immoral because there simply aren't any objective moral standards. That's all we're saying." With that he sat down.

"That's very interesting," Ted said, "and quite insightful, I must admit." He nodded his approval to the bookish young man. "And I'm going to surprise you by agreeing that if that is all you are saying, you can avoid this problem of self-refutation."

The questioner appeared pleased. But just then a conservative-looking older woman on the left side raised her hand. "You mean, that's all there is to it?" she shot back. "The problem is avoided that easily?"

"What do you mean, easily?" responded the young man, on his feet again, obviously not wanting to lose the ground he had gained.

"I mean you are getting off way too easily," the same woman responded, growing increasingly feisty. "You are the kind of person who wants to have your cake and eat it too. You know that certain things are wrong, really objectively wrong. You just won't admit it, and now you're trying to sidestep it with an explanation that you yourself probably don't even believe!"

The young man's mouth was open before she had even finished speaking. "There you go!" he burst out defiantly, not backing down one inch. "Imposing your view of morality on me, and even telling me that I know it's true. Well, I know nothing of the sort." As he spoke he grew more animated, waving his arms. "I'm sick and tired of these moralizers making moral judgments about my conduct and imposing their moral views on me when they have no business doing so. There is no basis for it, and they should stop it. It's that simple!"

A deafening silence filled the room. People stared nervously at each other. After a moment Ted spoke again. "Oh really?" he asked. "It's that simple?" He paused again. "It seems to me we've just seen an illustration of how *nonsimple* this matter is. Did you just say," he asked, turning to the young man, "that there is no basis for objective moral standards so we should"—he leaned on the word—"*should* stop

The distinction: difficult to maintain

making judgments about your conduct? Is that what you said?"

The young man paused, then shook his head ever so slightly. "Okay. Yes, I did, and I know what you're going to say."

"I'm sure you do. You just showed me and all these people how difficult it is to hold the moral subjectivist view without making at least one objective moral judgment. *Should* means 'ought.' You just did it.

"You just told me that because I have no basis for making objective moral judgments about your actions, I should—or ought—not make them."

The young man gave no response. He knew he had done exactly that.

"Let me repeat what I said to you a moment ago," Ted continued, "when you first claimed that you were arguing only that there is no rational basis for my making moral judgments about your actions. I agreed that if that is all you are saying, you can avoid my self-refutation problem.

"But you'll also recall that my earlier claim was that it is immensely difficult to do that. I believe those were my words. And, in fact, most moral subjectivists don't do only that. Most do what you just did. In practice they go further and tell us we *ought* not to pronounce moral judgment on their actions. And when they do so they refute their own position. Always remember the old adage: actions speak louder than words. That's true, of course, because our actions tell what we *really* believe."

With that, Ted stopped to let the import of these words register. Things had been tense, but now in the silence the audience began to relax, and the usual rustling of papers resumed.

Third problem: practical inconsistency — Ted continued. "But I said there were two difficulties to be encountered by those who argue morality is subjective. The second can be put this way: Is anyone really willing to live as though morality were all subjective? I doubt it.

"Consider the story of a philosophy student who wrote

an essay arguing that there were no objective moral principles. In terms of its research, structure, argumentation and documentation, it was a very strong paper. He slipped it into a shiny blue folder and handed it in. When it was returned the instructor had given it an F and written, 'I do not like blue folders.'

"Of course the student stormed back to the professor. 'You can't do this!' he yelled. 'It's not fair. How can you grade me on the basis of the color of my folder? If I wrote a good paper, I deserve a better grade.' "

People had stopped taking notes. Many were laughing as they guessed where the story was going.

Ted carried on with obvious enjoyment. "The instructor asked the student if he was referring to the paper that argued there are no objective standards such as fairness or justice. 'Yes, that's the one,' he responded. The instructor replied, 'Well, then, I don't like blue folders,' and went back to work."

Laughter filled the room. A group of older people in the back were the loudest.

"As the story goes," continued Ted, "once the instructor made his point, he changed the grade. But what was his point?" he asked very directly. "It was that the student had argued eloquently for subjective morality. He thought he believed it. But when it applied to *his* essay, he appealed to an objective standard that was correct regardless of what his instructor thought.

"In other words, he argued for moral subjectivism, but he didn't believe it either. Now, in my opinion," said Ted, leaning forward and speaking directly into the microphone, "that is a very damning charge. You see, it really is true that our actions often give us away. They tell the real story of what we believe. If it is true that a person does not consistently *live* as though moral values were subjective, then we have to say that neither does that person seriously *believe* they are subjective.

"The point we dare not miss about that story is that it pretty accurately depicts how every person claiming to believe that morality is subjective acts when an injustice is done to him or her. I would encourage you, as a practical project, to watch how anyone claiming to believe this acts when that person is lied to, cheated, defrauded or treated unfairly in some other way.

"Now, where have we come so far? We've seen some reasons why we ought not to think morality is subjective. It leads to consequences that are absurd or unacceptable, it is self-refuting, and virtually all will deny it when applied to themselves.

"Our next step will be to look at the other side of the coin and see the reasons why we ought to believe morality is objective. But now the master of ceremonies informs me that it is time for a short intermission and some refreshments, which I'm sure we're all ready for. You've been extremely attentive, and we've covered important ground. We'll see you after the break."

4

WHY MORALITY MUST BE OBJECTIVE

The Case for an Objective Moral Standard

C ould I have your attention, please?" The emcee's voice was barely audible above the talking and laughter. "I trust that rest and refreshment will take us through the second part of our evening. Before the break, Professor Douglas set out reasons why we ought not to think of morality as a strictly subjective commodity. From what he has said, it would be a mistake to view it this way.

"Now we need to know why we ought to consider morality an objective entity. And that is what he is about to tell us."

Most in the audience applauded as Ted walked to the

podium once again. A group on his right, however, sat quiet and stone-faced. One even booed. *Always a few dissenters,* Ted thought. *At least they're still here.*

A stranger in the back applauded. Though his applause was more subdued than most, his interest in the subject far surpassed that of the others.

Graham and Francine were still present and were anticipating the second half with great interest.

Opposing arguments support an alternative view

"Thank you!" Ted began. "It is always easier to criticize a view than to defend one.[1] We've just criticized the view that morality is subjective, and since there are just two alternatives, that criticism itself is a reason to think morality is objective. But can we say anything more in defense of this view? I think we can, so let's get started."

Papers shuffled as the note-takers readied themselves.

"I should point out," he continued, "that due to the nature of this issue some things we say now will overlap with ideas already covered before our break. But not to worry. Can I help it"—he laughed—"if a particular argument for objective morality also counts as one against subjective morality?"

Heads nodded.

"However," he went on, "when this occurs, we will be brief. Usually there is a new angle or perspective we won't want to miss.

The meaning of objective morality

"Let's begin with a precise statement of what we mean when we say morality is objective. We mean that our moral judgments are no longer like our judgments of personal taste. If morality is objective, we cannot say conflicting moral judgments are both right or that we are only speaking to ourselves when we make moral judgments. You'll recall that these are all concepts quite at home with the view that morality is subjective. None of them applies, however, when morality is considered to be objective.

"To say morality is objective is to say that there exists an objective entity independent of any human being. This entity we could call moral value, or moral truth, or a set of moral principles, or a moral standard if you will. What we call it is not important. What *is* important is that this moral truth is independent of any person. We don't determine or control it. It does not change from one person to another. Nor does it go away because we don't appreciate it. In fact, it is a very stubborn thing."[2]

"I've never heard it put that way before!" yelled out a man near the middle.

"But it's true, isn't it?" returned Ted. "Objective morality is simply there for us to discover and measure our actions against. Certain ones conform to it; these we call morally good acts. Others, the immoral ones, do not."

The man nodded his agreement, writing feverishly as he did.

Ted continued. "A comparison with something I said before the break might help clarify this. Earlier I said that if all morality is subjective, then the choice of whether to be a Mother Teresa or an Adolf Hitler was roughly the same as the choice of whether to be a saxophone player or an organ player."

At this statement, a young man near the front exploded. "Now that's a misrepresentation of our position! You're putting it in the worst possible light. Everyone knows that there is a genuine moral difference between the life of a Mother Teresa and that of an Adolf Hitler. You don't have to believe there is no difference simply because you are a moral subjectivist. You're trivializing the matter!" The young man was obviously agitated.

"Not in the least," replied Ted. "There is nothing trivial about it. It's true; we all know there is a difference between these two kinds of lifestyles, but my point is that if morality is purely subjective, as you obviously believe it is, then the choice between them will be morally arbitrary. There is no moral reason for choosing one over the other. Just go with whatever most appeals to you."

The young man listened, but said nothing though he was clearly displeased.

"However, if morality is objective," Ted continued, "none

The existence of a moral standard

of this is true anymore. There is now moral truth, or a moral standard, to be discovered. This moral standard judges that not all actions and courses of life are equal. Choosing to be an Adolf Hitler is no longer morally equivalent to choosing to be a Mother Teresa. The one is judged by this objective standard to be much better than the other."

The audience was silent. As Francine listened, she could see that this was an entirely new situation. What is more, she could see that there were consequences to viewing morality this way. But would she like those consequences? She was already becoming convinced that the consequences of subjective morality were impossible. How would these compare? But for now her only concern was with the reasons for viewing morality this way.

"But enough of clarifying what objective morality means!" exclaimed Ted. "Let's ask what reasons there are for thinking this objective standard really is there.

The basis for good and bad, better and worse

"Our first reason is straightforward enough," he began. "It is merely that the notion that all morality is purely subjective is grossly inadequate. To say that all moral judgments are equally correct is not satisfactory to any of us, because we know they are not all correct. That was made clear just a moment ago when all of us, objectivists and subjectivists, agreed that there really is a moral difference between the conduct of a Hitler and that of a Mother Teresa.

"But as we said earlier, if morality is completely subjective then we cannot condemn any action, however repugnant it appears to us. Why is that? It is because there is no such thing as morally better or worse. Things and actions aren't better than others, only different from them. Morally, all actions are equivalent.

A basis for moral progress

"But if that's the case, then there couldn't be any such thing as moral progress or improvement. How could there be if all courses of action are morally equivalent? Societies may change, but they would not improve or deteriorate, as the case may be.

"Now we saw this earlier, so I won't belabor it. I only want to make the point that this fact is also a reason for thinking morality is objective. Moral progress is possible only if morality is objective. Only then could one society be better or worse than another."

Suddenly a slight but feisty woman shouted from the back. "But how is that a reason for thinking morality is objective? Maybe there just is no such thing as moral progress." *A possible response*

"Good question," returned Ted, "and just when I wanted it. It is a reason for believing morality to be objective precisely because we all know intuitively that these facts are true. One society *can* be morally better or worse than another. We *know* it can. No one here today would argue that a society that discriminates, abuses and kills people purely on the basis of their race or skin color is morally equivalent to one that does not. What is more, there *is* such a thing as moral progress or deterioration over time. We know there is. Even if we don't know how we know it, the fact is we know it, and we know that we know it." *Universal moral knowledge*

Then he turned to the questioner. "As for your question, this is a reason for thinking morality is objective because there are only these two choices: either it is objective or it is subjective. If we reject one we are pushed to the only other alternative. And it looks as though we are going to have to reject the view that it is subjective."[3]

Ted looked at the woman and waited for a reply, but she had none, at least not yet. So he continued: "But let's go on to another reason. Actually, the next two reasons are only observations I will make about the way we speak and act. It seems that certain things we say and do give us away. They show beyond all reasonable doubt that we already do believe this objective standard is there. I'll make the observations, and you decide for yourselves whether they show what I think they do. I have a hunch, though, that we will all see that belief in this objective standard is such a basic part of our thinking that we couldn't imagine thinking without it. *What our actions tell about our views*

"Now I can hear some of you saying to yourselves right now: *How can it be this important in our thinking? We haven't even noticed it before. In fact, it's not until today that we even thought about the term 'objective moral value.'* "

"Right!" spoke up the feisty woman.

"I thought so," Ted quipped. "But that doesn't mean it's not there as part of how you think. In fact, it is precisely because it is such a fundamental part of our thinking process that we don't easily recognize it. It is in the background of our thought, an assumption that is there influencing the way we think but often unnoticed itself.

"Perhaps it's something like the law of noncontradiction. This law of logic states that a thing cannot both exist and not exist at the same time in the same sense. This object in my pocket cannot both be and not be a pen. At least not if we use the word *pen* the same way and refer to the same time. Now if you have never taken a course in logic you may never have heard of this law, but I can say with full assurance that you all believe it nonetheless. In fact, it asserts great influence over the way you think and act. It is an assumption operating at a very foundational level in your thought.[4]

What quarreling says about objective morality

"But let's get back to this objective moral standard. What observations do you suppose I could make to show that we already believe this standard is there? Well, let me ask you this: have you ever watched two people argue? I mean really get into it, a good quarrel? And have you ever analyzed what's really going on when a good argument is under way?"

Some snickered at the question, but most stared blankly, wondering where the professor was going with it. "Well, let's do that right now. When people argue, don't they say something like this: 'Hey, you can't do that; that's not fair,' or 'That just isn't decent,' or 'Give that back—I had it first'? Others may say, 'But you promised,' or 'How would you like it if someone did that to you?' or 'Leave her alone; she isn't hurting you.' "

Heads were nodding in response.

"So you've said them too?" he smiled.

An older couple looked at each other sheepishly. Ted bit his tongue.

"True confessions," he added. "Of course you've made these comments and others like them. So have I. And who hasn't? That is precisely my point. This is how humans argue.

"But think carefully about what each of these statements is saying. They are not merely saying we don't like what the other person is doing. Of course that's included, but they are saying more than that. They are appealing to a standard of conduct which we are saying the other person has violated. What's more, we expect the other person already to know about this standard, don't we? Never do we feel the need to ask, 'By the way, have you heard of fairness? How about decency? And what do you think of breaking promises?' "

By this time the audience was laughing at Ted's questions, but the fact that they laughed showed how true his point was.

He continued. "We expect the other person to know. And notice what follows next. Never does the other person stand in amazement, wondering why you would appeal to this standard. Nor does she say, 'But who cares about fairness, or decency, or keeping promises?' Rather, she usually tries to show that her conduct really did somehow conform to that standard. It really was fair or decent. If you really understood the whole situation, she will say, you would know that. Something has happened that lets this person out of keeping her promise. The point is that the conduct fits with the standard, or so she will argue.[5]

"The important observation we are making from this quick analysis is that both arguers appear to have in mind an independent, objective standard of morality on which they agree. And they do. If they didn't, they couldn't argue as we all do. Furthermore, they are not afraid to impose the standard on others.

"In fact, we could almost define an argument, in the non-technical sense, as the attempt to show that another person is wrong. And this cannot be done unless there is some fundamental agreement on what real right and wrong are."

Ted went on. "It is almost as if part of being human is to recognize this objective moral standard. We all know it, and we assume everyone else knows it too. It's a foundational part of our thinking. Common everyday human activities such as arguing could not be carried out without the widespread assumption that objective moral value exists. We don't need to be taught it.

"Let's imagine that others didn't know about this standard. Then all the nasty things we've said about people like Hitler, Idi Amin or others would make no sense. What is the point in condemning them if they have no basic moral sense that those actions are wrong? If they don't, we cannot blame them for those actions any more than for their height or skin color."

The room fell quiet.

"Now it's important to add here that saying we all *recognize* this objective standard is not the same as saying we all *keep* it all of the time. The fact is, we don't. None of us. And that sometimes makes us uneasy, because this moral standard is most inflexible. It condemns us when we violate it and affirms us when we don't. But recognize it we do.[6]

"Well, that is one observation that shows we already believe this standard is there. It's also my second reason for believing morality is an objective reality rather than a subjective one.

Moral subjectivism's practical inconsistency

"There is a third reason for this contention," Ted continued. "It too is an observation, but not about all of us."

There was a shuffle of papers as the note-takers readied new sheets.

"Let's think," he continued, "about the person who argues that there really is no objective moral standard. And let's ask an important question about her: How does she respond when someone breaks a promise to her, treats her unfairly or harms her without provocation?

"Now here is a remarkable thing!" Ted exclaimed. "The same person who denies there is any objective moral standard one moment goes back on her word the next. She will immediately accuse you of acting unfairly or indecently or dishonestly toward her."

Many in the audience began to smile.

"It looks like she has let the cat out of the bag on this point," he continued. "She has shown that, whatever she may say, she too recognizes this objective standard just like everyone else.

"But," he concluded, "this only shows that, as hard as a person may try, no one can escape objective moral values. It reminds me of that story I told earlier about the student with the essay in the blue folder. He tried to avoid an objective standard, but in the end he couldn't.

"There is yet one more observation to make, and this one concerns all of us. We will see that it merely confirms what we've already seen about human behavior."

One student, frustrated by the audience's willingness to yield to the lecturer, walked out.

"You will remember," Ted continued, ignoring the interruption, "that we've already admitted that none of us keeps this moral law we're talking about all the time. We know that. However, notice what we—and I mean all of us, including me—usually do when we violate it. Don't we immediately think up a list of excuses for our behavior? The longer the better. Excuses like 'But I couldn't help it,' 'You should have seen what she did to me last weekend' or 'That serves you right—you've never treated me honestly.' "

Our excuses: another evidence of an objective moral standard

He could see a group of young people grinning nervously at each other and could hardly hold back from making a comment to them.

"Now the point is not," he went on, "that these are good excuses. Some, in fact, are pretty flimsy. We ourselves would never accept them from someone else.

"Rather, the point is that the very fact that we make them

at all is just one more evidence of how deeply entrenched in our minds is the belief in an objective moral standard. You see, if there is no such thing as decent or fair or honest behavior, why are we so busy making excuses for behaving unfairly or indecently or dishonestly? The fact that we make excuses shows that we recognize that this standard is there. In fact, we feel its force on us so strongly that we can't bear the thought that we are breaking it, and we try to justify our behavior to it.

"Let me conclude this point," he added, looking up from his notes and speaking directly into the microphone, "by affirming once again that the existence of this objective standard seems inescapable. We all know it exists. Indeed, it seems pointless to try to disprove it. Either objective moral truth is there or a large part of normal human conduct makes no sense. It becomes irrational."

A calm had settled over the audience. This had been an idea-packed evening. As Ted looked out he could tell that, for quite a few, many of these ideas had been new. For at least one they had been—for whatever reason—too much.

As Graham and Francine thought over Ted's lecture, many ideas were running through their minds. On one hand, many of tonight's ideas were familiar ones. Sure, they often appealed to certain standards when they quarreled. They knew that. Yes, they expected others to know about them. Of course they were painfully aware of their own moral deficiencies.

However, one of those familiar ideas had touched a raw nerve with Francine. She had already recalled with particular agony the lineup of excuses she had made just last week for not keeping her promise to deliver some parcels for her neighbor. It seemed so trivial at the time. But why had she made those excuses if there was nothing to it?

But what was especially new in tonight's lecture was what all these familiar ideas meant for the existence of an objective moral standard. It was pretty clear, thought Francine, that if normal human behavior was rational and made any sense at all, there must be objective moral values. You couldn't have one without the other.

But at the same time, some things bothered Francine about this standard. Where did it come from? Where is it now? How do we know about it? What about the differing moral ideas various people and cultures seem to have?

Her thoughts were interrupted by the sound of Ted's voice. "This has been a mental marathon," he said sympathetically. "I'm impressed by your interest and attentiveness. Earlier I had said there would be time for questions."

Perfect! thought Francine. She knew that unless there were answers to these and other questions, it would be difficult to believe morality was really objective.

Ted continued. "But first we'll take a well-deserved break. Unwind and prepare your questions. Please have them thought out succinctly. We'll regroup momentarily."

Common questions concerning objective morality

5
HEY, I OBJECT!
Obstacles to Believing in Objective Morality

The master of ceremonies was calling the audience to order. "We're now at that part of the evening," he boomed, "that we've all been waiting for." He was, of course, referring to the question period Ted had promised. "The rule is that virtually anything goes here: questions, clarifications and disagreements. They're all welcome. But please, no lectures or speeches. Just state your question as succinctly as you can."

One man at the back had some questions, but he wanted to remain unseen by the lecturer. *Maybe,* he thought to himself, *my questions will be answered in the coming weeks.*

His thoughts were cut short by the first question from an older, balding gentleman sitting close to one of the floor microphones. As he rose, it was clear that he disagreed with Ted's conclusions. He spoke slowly and deliberately. "You speak of this objective moral standard," he started, "as something out there, distinct from us. We just recognize it?"

"That is correct."

"Well, I disagree." He was obviously annoyed.

"I can see that," returned Ted. *Nothing like a little controversy to heat up the evening,* he thought to himself.

The audience was clearly enjoying it as well. Many were looking back at the questioner. "But please go ahead," Ted continued. "This is your opportunity. Make your case. Maybe it's better than mine."

Objection: "objective morality" is merely instinct

The questioner asked, "Have you ever considered the possibility that maybe there is no objective standard out there? Maybe we are simply prompted by instinct," he said with great emphasis on those last two words, "to call certain things right and others wrong. I mean we obviously have other instincts: a fear instinct, a sexual instinct, an instinct for food, just to name a few. We have them for survival. Couldn't we also have developed what we could call a moral instinct for the same purpose, for survival?"

With that the questioner sat down. There was silence, not to mention a certain tension in the air. Then Ted looked up and said, "I must say, that is a very astute question, and a fair one—assuming there is such a thing as real fairness." He grinned.

Some in the audience chuckled.

"But let's not get sidetracked," he added. "I would assume this questioner believes there is real fairness, in which case he already believes in this objective standard I'm talking about.

"But back to his actual question. First, let me agree with you, sir." He spoke directly to the questioner. "We do have instincts, and we have them for survival. However, I must make a critically important distinction here that will shed light on this question. The distinction is between our instincts on the one hand and our sense that certain things are right and wrong on the other hand.

Defining our instincts

"Let's ask what we mean when we say we are prompted

by instinct. We mean that we have a powerful desire, an impulse to do a certain thing, do we not?" he asked. "Now, I admit that sometimes we have just that kind of desire to do something good or helpful for another person. We could call that our social or herd instinct, if you will.

"That is instinct. But that is not what we mean when we speak of our moral sense. We don't mean that we have a desire to do certain things. We mean we sense that we *ought* to do certain things whether or not we desire them. We have a sense of duty to do them.

Distinguishing our moral sense from instinct

"In fact," Ted continued, "we all know that there are times when this sense of duty conflicts with our instincts. Your sexual instinct may urge you to have an extramarital sexual encounter, but your moral sense tells you that you ought not to because of a promise you made to your spouse. Clearly, this moral sense is not one of your instincts. Instincts function as desires, not as a sense of 'ought.'

"But there's another way we can see the moral sense functioning differently from our impulses. Sometimes it stands behind our impulses and judges between them. When we see someone in need, we often have conflicting instincts. One, our social instinct, makes us want to help. Another, our fear instinct, says, *Get out of here! This could be dangerous!* But then, behind these two impulses, is a third thing, our moral sense. It is different from either of them, since it is not itself an instinct. It tells us which instinct we ought to follow. It acts as a judge between the two instincts.

"To sum up, it looks as if this recognition that things are really right or wrong is a different thing from our survival instincts."[1]

The next question came from a student with a mature air. *Probably a graduate student,* Ted thought to himself. He was clearly confident, even a little cocky.

"Professor," he began, "we've been sitting here listening to you make your case for these objective moral principles. Very interesting, I have to admit, and I suppose that through argument you could show that white is black and black is white."

"Aren't you overrating the power of argumentation just a little?" interrupted Ted.

"A little, maybe. But you have used arguments to make this idea of an objective moral standard sound reasonable, even believable. However, as far as I'm concerned it's a very bizarre notion. It's absurd." The man was becoming animated as he spoke, his voice rising.

Common questions about an objective moral standard He continued. "I mean, there are some important questions you seem to be ignoring. For instance, what are these objective principles? You speak as if this is all clear, but it isn't. And where are they? How do we come to know them?

"The whole thing is far-fetched!" he shouted, waving his right arm. With that he sat down.

The audience was silent, momentarily taken aback at his outburst. Francine was pleased, since the man had voiced some of her own questions. Ted broke the silence, himself a little animated as well. "So you think it's bizarre?"

"Very!" the young man shot back from his seat.

"And I take it that it's the unanswered questions that make it bizarre?"

Without backing down an inch, the student called out, "Well, if we don't know what these principles are, where they are or how we know them, doesn't that qualify as bizarre at best and absurd at worst?"

Some in the audience snickered.

"Well, now," said Ted, rolling up his sleeves. "Suppose we were able to answer these questions. Would that make it a sensible, reasonable concept for you?" He waited for a response.

"You'll never convince me!" responded the student emphatically.

"Possibly not, but let's see if there are answers to your questions. You must admit that if we can do that, your reason for saying an objective moral standard is absurd no longer stands."

The student looked defiant but said nothing.

"I believe you've raised three questions about these objective moral principles: What are they? Where are they? How do we know them? I think these are more easily answered than you might suppose.

"First, I think we already know what they are. Think of the UN Declaration of Human Rights. Also the ancient moral codes I spoke of earlier. And don't forget what I noted about the way people argue. These all show that human beings have always agreed on certain moral ideas. I think we agree on them today. Let me ask you: Is fairness good or bad? Is truth something to be valued? Is it good to respect human life? What about respect for parents? Is it right or wrong to torture human beings without cause?"

What are these objective moral standards?

Laughter could be heard throughout the room.

"So you laugh at those questions. And you should—but your laughter is quite revealing. It tells us just how well we all know these moral truths. Even the idea that we would need to ask about them strikes us as funny.

"But that throws light on your second question," Ted said directly to the graduate student. "You ask how we know them. When you think about it, it may not matter much how we know them, just that we do. And we've already seen that if there is anything that is certain about human beings, it is that we know what these moral principles are.

How do we learn about objective moral standards?

"In fact we know them so well that we almost consider this knowledge a part of being human. What would you think of an individual who seemed to have no compunction about torturing, maiming, enslaving or killing others? And when we asked him to stop, suppose he was genuinely surprised and annoyed that anyone would make such a request. At best, we would probably call that person a defective human being. We might even question his humanness altogether. But whatever we decided on that, the fact is that this kind of person is virtually nonexistent.

"Clearly, we know about these moral principles. The only thing we can say about how we come to know them is that the knowledge of them has been infused into the human psyche. It's there in all of us."

The graduate student was sitting down by now, arms folded. So far he was content to listen without reply, but that was not to last for long.

Where are objective moral standards?

Ted turned directly to him and said, "A quick comment on your third question. I believe you were asking where these moral principles are."

He nodded but said nothing.

"I'll have to answer this question by asking you one as well: do you have rights?"

"Of course I do!"

"Where are they?"

"Huh? I mean . . ."

"Do you have privileges?" Ted interrupted.

"Yes." He was clearly uneasy.

"Where are they?"

"Okay, I see what you are trying to prove," responded the graduate student. "However, those words *rights* and *privileges* are only terms I use to say I am allowed to do certain things unhindered by others. By using them I'm not referring to anything existing out there somewhere." He pointed vaguely toward the ceiling.

"Exactly. But aren't you referring to something real, something that does not depend on how others feel about your having this right?"

"Okay, I'll grant you that."

"And that is precisely what we mean when we speak of objective moral principles. We mean that certain acts are commendable while others are wrong and ought not to be done. And the fact that they are commendable or condemnable does not depend upon how anyone feels about the matter. It is not subject to the whims of any individual person or group of people.

"To ask where these principles are is to make a category mistake. It is like asking where your objective rights and privileges are. Or how heavy is the color red. Or what color is the musical note C."

Ted could see people laughing at the questions, and their laughter illustrated his point. "It's the wrong question," he continued, "and of course it can't be answered. But that does not change the fact that objective moral standards do exist and we know what they are."[2]

The next questioner was a woman on the far right side of the auditorium. She asked her question cordially but earnestly.

"Thank you for the lecture. I found it very interesting. Convincing too," she added.

"Thank you," interrupted Ted. "So far I like your question very much."

Laughter erupted throughout the room.

"Yes, yes," she continued, "but there's more."

"Somehow I thought there might be," he quipped.

"There is just one thing," she went on, "that bothers some of us here." She pointed to a group of friends sitting nearby. "At one point you stated that everyone inherently recognizes and knows about this objective moral standard. No one needs to be taught such principles as fairness, decency, honesty, etc."

Ted nodded.

"But," she went on, "isn't it precisely the other way around? Aren't we all taught by our parents and others that these principles are good and the opposite principles bad? Don't parents teach these ideas to their children at a very early age? It seems to me that they do and that these principles become internalized in their minds. In fact, they become almost a part of them. Like any good habit, they become automatic so that we don't need to establish them when we argue with others.

Objection: aren't moral standards merely learned from others?

"As you say," she continued, "we can assume the other person knows about them, but couldn't this be because she too has been taught these principles and has internalized them?"

With that she sat down and waited for his reply.

"I must say," he began, "that is one of the foremost objections to the idea of an objective moral standard. You have put it well."

She laughed good-naturedly.

"The objection is," he went on, "that we do not get these moral principles from any objective moral standard. Rather, we are all taught them by our parents and teachers. The fact that they are taught to us may rule out the existence of this objective standard. Is that a fair restatement of your question?"

She nodded affirmingly.

"First," he continued, "let me say that I agree, we *are* taught certain moral principles by our parents and others. You are absolutely right about that. The critical question is what this fact tells us about morality.

"If I could be so bold, however, I would like to point out a misunderstanding behind this objection. Actually, it's an assumption you seem to be making which I think we ought not to make."

The questioner nodded slowly, leaning forward to catch every word.

Ideas we learn,
not necessarily
human inventions

Ted went on. "I think you are assuming that if we learned an idea from another human being, then that idea must be nothing more than a human invention. It originated with humans and could have been thought up differently from the way it is. Like the idea that a red light means stop and a green one means go. Humans thought that up. They could have decided green means stop."

"Exactly!"

"But," he said, "there's a problem with that assumption, isn't there? If you think about it, not all the things we have learned from other humans are human inventions that could have been different from what they are."

"You've lost me," the young woman admitted. "Why not?"

"Look at it this way," he answered. "Isn't it true that some things that we learn from others are not human inventions at all? Humans teach them but don't invent them. They are things that could not be different from what they are. For example, think of basic logical truths such as 'a whole is greater than any of its parts' or 'a thing cannot both exist and not exist in the same sense at the same time.' Or think also of mathematical truths such as five times seven equals thirty-five.

"Now, clearly, these are truths that young students learn at school from their teachers. A child who grew up with a pack of animals would never be taught them; he or she might not ever learn them. But does it follow that human beings invented these ideas or that they could be different from what they are? Clearly not. We only recognize them as truths that exist apart from us and simply pass them along to our children and students."

"Yes," the questioner replied. "Some ideas do seem to be like that."

"So what we've come to," Ted went on, "is that there are really two kinds of things we learn. First, there are what some have called 'real truths.'[3] These are the ones that exist apart from human beings. We simply recognize them and pass them along. They could not be different from what they are. The second category consists of ideas that are merely human inventions. These are the ideas that humans have thought up and that might have been different. We could call these social conventions, if you wish."

Two kinds of learned ideas: real truths and human inventions

He paused for a moment, then asked the questioner if she was following him so far.

"I think so," she responded. "Your green light, red light example fits in the second category. Am I right?"

"Precisely. As do all traffic laws. We have decided in North America that a red light means stop and a green one means go. There is no reason why it couldn't have been the other way round or, for that matter, that two different colors couldn't have been chosen—say, blue and purple. We have also decided that all drivers must drive on the right-hand side of the road. There is no reason we couldn't have chosen the left. In fact, in England that is precisely what they chose, and from what we hear it works just as well."

"I've been there," she laughed. "Actually, I prefer their system, but you do have to get used to it."

"There you go. A social convention, pure and simple. But let's not miss the point in all of this. These ideas are entirely different from mathematical or logical truths, even though both are learned from others. These we make up rather than simply recognize. What is more, these social conventions could be different from what they are."[4]

"So then," said a young man near the questioner, rising to his feet, "you have distinguished between these two kinds of ideas—social conventions and real truths." He raised his arms, one at a time, to help show the distinction.

"Right," affirmed Ted.

"And both kinds of ideas are learned?"

"Right again."

The young man paused to look at his notes. "The social conventions we invent, but the real truths we merely recognize?"

"You're putting it well."

"But there's still something missing here," the young man went on. "I assume you think that these moral principles that we learn from others belong to the class of real truths and not the other group."

"Yes, I do," answered Ted.

Objective moral standards: real truths

"But don't you have to show that?" queried the young man. "I mean, why should any of us think that? Why couldn't I just as easily believe these moral principles are like social conventions?"

"Excellent!" Ted said exuberantly. "You're one step ahead of us. Yes, we do have to show why moral principles are more like real truths than social conventions. And I believe there is good reason for thinking this. Let me explain.

The similarity among objective moral truths

"Unlike social conventions, which can and do change, the moral principles we're talking about appear to be fundamentally similar wherever we find humanity. They don't change from person to person over time. Have you ever wondered why whenever and wherever you meet another human being, you can automatically assume that she will recognize certain moral principles to be true and others false?

"In other words, these moral principles function like real truths, not social conventions. There is a fundamental similarity in moral principles anywhere we choose to look, just as with mathematical and logical truths. Whether it be in our society or another, certain things are valued: fairness, decency, honesty, respect for human life and other concepts. The opposite principles are condemned.

"My point here is that if they were nothing but social conventions, surely there would be fundamental differences, as there are among other social conventions, between various groups of people. We would expect this even more in light of all the other differences between various groups of people—differences in climate, background, level of development, location and so on. But the remarkable feature of human morality is not the small differences between groups of people but the fundamental similarities between them.

"Furthermore, if they were simply social conventions, then they could be changed at will any time it suited enough people, and no one would think anything of it. But have you noticed what we do when we come across a person or group of people who act as though moral principles can be changed at will—who treat them like social conventions, in other words?

Our resistance to changes in moral standards

"What did we do with the Nazis and their concentration camps? What do we do with our neighbors who blatantly break their promises to us? We condemn them as either morally corrupt or morally ignorant. Either way, we treat these principles very much as though they were real truths. We seem to say, 'If you don't know about these principles, you should. And if you don't follow them, you ought to!' "

The young man was nodding in agreement. "That is how we treat them," he responded.

Moral truth: recognized but not invented

"Yes, it is!" exclaimed Ted. "It looks then like we human

beings are teaching these truths and yet we are not inventing them. They are already there. We are merely recognizing them and teaching them to our children, who in turn give them a ready acceptance because deep within their psyches, they too, as they grow to maturity, recognize them to be really true."

"Thank you!" replied the young questioner. "I'll need time to think more on that."

"Please do!" Ted smiled. "As I said, your question is a critical one. We must be able to show that moral principles are real truths."

A bright crowd, Ted thought to himself. Good questions so far. He knew, however, that one especially contentious issue had not yet been raised. Could the entire evening pass without it? *That would be unbelievable,* he thought. And he was right.

6
BUT DON'T DIFFERENT CULTURES HAVE DIFFERENT MORAL PRACTICES?
A Major Obstacle to Objective Morality

The next question came from a young, athletic man on Ted's left. He was picking up from the previous questioner.

"Thank you for your answer to the last question," he began. "There is just one thing bothering me about it."

"And that is . . . ?"

"Your reason for believing certain moral principles are real truths."

"My reason?" queried Ted.

"Yes," said the young man. "You believe they are real truths and not social conventions because they are held by all people everywhere."

"Uh-huh."

"And because of a fundamental similarity in the moral principles held by all people. Am I right?"

"You've listened well," replied Ted.

Objection: different moral practices contradict the notion of an objective moral standard
"Well, here is what bothers me," said the young man, pausing to collect his thoughts. "I don't see it that way. It seems to me that the exact opposite is the case. I mean, isn't it true that different people, groups and societies around the world have strikingly *different* moral practices from ours? Don't anthropologists give reports of practices that we would condemn?"

Ted was nodding in agreement.

"Well, then, how can there be this one objective standard that all people recognize?"[1] With that the young man sat down and waited for a response.

Ted had to admit he was impressed. This was the other notorious objection to the existence of an objective moral standard. He had wondered if it would come up tonight, and here it was.

"Great question," he began. "And, I might add, well put!"

The young man smiled.

"First, let me say, you are right. There are certain differences in the moral practices of various groups around the world. But let's think about these for a moment. Have you also considered the very different circumstances, conditions and social contexts we find people in around the globe?"

The relevance of differences in people's circumstances
The young man hadn't. Nor had he expected this kind of response. He craned his neck forward, unsure of where this professor was going with his last question.

"When we look at various societies and cultures in the world, we find differences in history, climate, technological development, educational and social development, and material prosperity, to name a few.

"Now, given these differences," Ted went on, "the remarkable thing is not how different various peoples' moral practices are but how similar they are.

"Let's imagine what a strikingly different moral practice, as *Illustrations of* you called it, would be like. Imagine living among a group of *radically different* people where you were commended for deceiving your friends *moral practices* and neighbors without cause."

He paused to let this sink in.

"Or for making a promise to your neighbor with the clear intention of breaking it. Or for withholding from your friend what was clearly his for no reason at all. That would be a strikingly different morality.

"Of course, these things happen even in our society, but the person doing them does not receive commendation. In fact, he is condemned. Ask yourself who the heroes are in the movies you watch. Are they the people who rape, murder, brutalize, deceive and break their promises?"

Ted could see from the expressions of the audience that he was getting through to them.

"You know they're not. And so do I. What politician runs for office without telling us how honest and fair she is and how she will keep her promises and has done so in the past? But imagine a society where to get elected you had to brag about the number of people you had deceived, the promises you'd broken, the items you'd stolen? *That* would be a strikingly different morality."

"No thanks!" shouted an older man from the back.

"My point exactly!" Ted shot back. "We can't imagine it and certainly wouldn't want it.

"Now I must add that I am referring here to normal, every- *The way to* day conduct, not merely to exceptional behavior in unusual *understand* situations. We all have our exceptions where we allow—even *moral conduct* commend—behavior that we would normally condemn. In our society we commend spying on others' private activities in wartime. We send police informants into drug rings to build friendships so as to gain trust and information for the express purpose of double-crossing the one whose trust has been gained. We do that here, and other societies have their own similar exceptional activities.

"But even here we do not believe actions like spying or double-crossing are morally good in themselves. They are given temporary, qualified approval when they are seen as the only means to avoid some greater evil. We sanction actions like these only in unusual circumstances when not doing so would lead to an even worse situation, such as a military victory by a tyrant.

"These are the exceptions, and I am not referring to them. You do not prove one society's morality is different from another's by pointing to exceptions in one's morality. Every society has its own exceptions. I am thinking of a society where this kind of activity is the norm. You see, it is these strikingly different moral practices that we don't find."

Heads nodded slowly throughout the room.

"In fact," Ted added, "what we do find are fundamental similarities in value systems around the world."

Demonstrations of the fundamental similarity in moral views

Then he asked, "How many have heard of the Universal Declaration of Human Rights?"

A few hands went up.

"Well, it provides a simple yet strong demonstration of this fundamental similarity in value systems all around the world. This document was drawn up by the United Nations in 1948 and signed by many nations. And here's the point. Certain kinds of conduct are labeled in the strongest of terms as morally right and obligatory, while others are condemned.[2]

"Considering it is signed by nations all around the world, it is a remarkably specific document. Human freedom, dignity, life, liberty, security and many other things are said to be morally good. Racial and gender discrimination, slavery, arbitrary arrest, torture, all forms of degrading treatment and other acts are condemned.

"What is more, it doesn't matter much what time period we consider here. This UN document is relatively modern. But from as far back as we have moral codes recorded, we see fundamental similarities. The English writer C. S. Lewis has done us a great service in compiling a list of ancient moral codes so as to highlight fundamental similarities between them.[3]

"The moral imperative against murder or cruel treatment of other human beings is found in the moral codes of the ancient Egyptians, Jews, Babylonians, Hindus and Chinese. The command to honor and respect parents, elders and ancestors is found in the moral codes of the ancient Hindus, Babylonians, Greeks, Jews, Egyptians and Chinese. Values such as honesty, mercy and care for children are likewise found in a wide spectrum of ancient codes.

"The point in all of this," said Ted, looking up from his materials, "is this. Considering the radically different situations we find people in, it is not the differences in moral practices that are remarkable. It is the similarities.

"This all goes to reinforce my main contention. There really is one objective moral standard. All people, wherever and in whatever condition they find themselves, recognize this standard. In other words, this is precisely what we would expect to find if an objective standard existed: fundamental similarities with minor differences due to different conditions in life."

There was silence as he gave time for the listeners to absorb this point.

Then the silence was broken by the same young man. Rising to his feet again, he said, "Professor, I agree that the similarities in moral practice are great. But with all due respect, are there not still *some* differences?"[4]

Specific differences in moral practice explored

There was a ripple of laughter at his persistence.

"Yes, there are. I don't deny it."

"I thought so, but how can there be if what you say is true?" pressed the young man. "If all people recognize and are guided by this set of objective moral principles, as you say, how can *any* different moral practices exist?"

"Well stated!" exclaimed Ted, "because that is the question we must ask. If there are objective moral principles, how then can we account for any genuinely different moral practices we may find? And the first thing to say about it is that it is one thing to recognize or know about an objective moral standard. It is quite another to follow and obey it. I have not argued that

Knowing a moral standard is different from living by it

all people actually obey the moral principles they know all the time. In fact, none of us does this all the time.

"But that means it is possible that when we find certain people who do things we condemn, they are acting in violation of moral standards that they know full well. They know the standard. They just don't live by it."

"Hmm. I can see how that could be the case sometimes," the young man responded. "But aren't there societies that, with no thought of wrongdoing, carry out practices that we condemn?"

Ted nodded, his eyebrows raised. Then, turning to the young man, he said, "There may be. Perhaps you have an example in mind."

The young man paused, whispering briefly to the person sitting beside him. Then looking up he smiled sheepishly and said, "Yes, I do."

The audience laughed at his resourcefulness.

"It's nice to have your research assistants with you," joked Ted.

"Yes, it is," he grinned. "The example I'm thinking of is of the Eskimo people. Anthropologists have found that in the past infanticide was quite common. They would leave their infant children, especially girls, out to freeze to death. This was permitted completely at the parents' discretion. No social stigma was attached to it. Yet we would abhor such a practice."[5]

"Thank you," responded Ted. "I too am aware of that practice and have thought much about it. So what are we to make of a practice that is so different from conduct we believe to be acceptable? When we consider practices different from our own, just like this one, a critically important question must be asked. You'll want to follow me carefully here."

The young man nodded his agreement.

Different practices, not necessarily different moral values

"We must ask not only *what* actions people perform but *why* they perform them," he continued. "The reason for their actions becomes all-important. We have to realize that a difference in moral *practice* may not always be because of a difference in moral *values* or *principles* held by the people. There are at least a couple of other reasons why people may perform practices different from some other group."

He could see inquisitive looks on many faces.

"As I said, please stick with me, and I promise you it will become clearer. Different practices may be due to a difference in a group's circumstances or conditions in life. Or they may be the result of different beliefs about reality. Let's explain further and illustrate.

The relevance of different circumstances to the morality of actions

"Take the first difference I just mentioned, the difference in a group's circumstances or conditions in life. It is possible that a group of people could have the same moral values or principles as we have and yet"—he paused briefly—"because of vastly different circumstances in life, those values cause them to perform different actions from what we do—actions that would appear morally abhorrent to us until we understood why they do them."

The note-takers were writing feverishly. One bold young woman near the front spoke up: "I hope you have an example!"

"Let's consider the one given by the previous questioner, the Eskimo practice of infanticide," answered Ted. "You see, upon first hearing of this practice, it could sound like these people do not love their children as we do or that they do not have the respect for human life that we have. In other words, it sounds like they have radically *different moral values* from ours."

"That's obvious!" exclaimed the young man. "We would never do such a thing."

Many nodded their agreement. All listened intently.

"Let's face it. In our society there would be a great social stigma attached to such a practice. Anyone who kills his children is locked up for a good long time.

"But suppose we get to our important question and ask why these people did this. Did they really love their children less than we do? Did they have less respect for human life than we do? Or could it be that they simply had different circumstances that forced them into such a practice? You see, until we answer that question, we can't say for sure that they are following different moral values from ours, can we?"

He paused, giving this concept time to take hold.

"And when we take a closer look," he continued, "we do in fact find very different circumstances. We find no reason to think the Eskimos did not protect their children to the extent that conditions would permit. Just like us. But they lived in a harsh environment. Food was often in short supply. Furthermore, mothers often breastfed their babies much longer, up to four years. Even in the best of times, the number of infants a family could raise was limited.

"In addition, the Eskimos were a nomadic people, unable to farm. This meant they were always on the move in search of food. Infants had to be carried, and a mother could carry only one in her parka. In other words, these people lived on the margin of existence. We don't. Which means we will have some difficulty putting ourselves in their shoes."

Ted paused briefly, and then an idea struck him. "Let's try a little exercise. Ask yourselves these question: What if I had more children than I could support? What if I knew one was going to die because there simply was no way to keep that child alive? What if neither I nor my society had the means to care for all my children? What would I, or you for that matter, do in that situation—we who love our children and claim to have a high regard for human life?"

Then he stopped and waited for his audience to answer in their own minds. He realized full well the seriousness of the question. Not a sound could be heard.

"Would we not," he went on, "search out the most painless, humane way to bring about a child's death precisely because we do love our children and because we do respect human life? I think we might. That is what the Eskimos did. Freezing to death is a relatively painless way to die. The child falls into a deep sleep and then dies in its sleep.

"I should point out that this is not parallel to the young woman in our society who becomes pregnant and cannot imagine how she will ever support a baby so decides to abort it or put it in a garbage bag to die after it is born. The difference is that there are resources in our society she could draw on if she chose, but she is *unwilling* to do that. She is choosing to abort her child or kill it after it is born when she wouldn't actually have to. The Eskimo people, on the other hand, had no resources to turn to. They knew that these extra children *would* die. There was no way to prevent that. Precisely because of their love for those children and their respect for human life, they looked for the most humane, painless way to bring about what they knew was inevitable anyway."

The young man was on his feet again. "Are you defending their practice?" he asked.

"It may sound like it," Ted replied.

"There's an understatement!"

"But actually I'm not."

The young man's mouth dropped.

"Let me be crystal-clear on exactly what I am claiming. My main contention here is not that this practice was morally good but that it does not necessarily prove that the Eskimos held *different* moral values from what we hold. In other words, if we found ourselves in the same kind of situation as them, we would probably do the same. That was the original question, remember? Why are there such *different* moral practices in the world?"

The young man signaled that he remembered.

"What we should learn from this is that among the Eskimo people, infanticide did not signal a fundamentally different attitude toward children. Instead, they recognized that at times harsh measures were necessary to ensure the survival of the family. What is more, it was precisely because of their love for their children and their respect for human life that they looked for the most humane and painless way for them to die. You see," Ted said, looking at the young questioner, "the raw data of the anthropologists can be misleading."

"But isn't there still something missing here?" interjected the young man, rising to his feet once again. "I agree, you have shown how differences in circumstances led these people to practice infanticide. But why more baby girls than boys?

The necessity of
asking why
people act as
they do

Doesn't that signal a difference in values from us?"

"It would appear that way," said Ted, "until we again ask why. And when we do, we are led to two facts about their circumstances. First, in their society males were the primary food providers, the hunters. This was how they traditionally divided the work up. Obviously, if they were to survive as a people, it was necessary to maintain a sufficient number of men.

"Second, because the hunters suffered a high casualty rate, the adult men who died far outnumbered the women who died early. Thus if male and female infants survived in equal numbers, the female adult population would far outnumber the male adults.

"In other words, it doesn't look like they killed more female babies than males because they loved or respected them less. This was simply one of the harsh measures necessary for survival as a people.

"My point in all of this is that sometimes what appears to be a difference in morality is really a difference in circumstances. The same moral principles operating in vastly different circumstances can produce very different actions."

At this point Ted stopped. All the talking had made him thirsty, and he took a drink of water. He was glad for his audience's attentiveness, because he knew that differences in people's circumstances could account for many differences in moral practices in the world. But it could not account for all of them. More needed to be said.

He was just about to proceed when he noticed a hand raised near the back of the auditorium. "Didn't you mention something earlier," said a middle-aged man, rising to his feet, "about another kind of difference?"

"Thank you, yes I did!" responded Ted happily. "And we need that difference right now."

The relevance of
different beliefs
about reality for
the morality of
actions

"Wasn't it a difference"—the man paused to look at his notes—"in people's beliefs about reality?"

"That's right."

"Well, some of us here"—the man pointed to a group of

people sitting nearby—"are wondering what you mean by that. And I believe you said that, whatever it is, it could also account for certain differences in moral practice."

"That is what I said," Ted confirmed. "Let me illustrate what I mean by a difference in a person's beliefs about reality. I think we'll see it's quite a simple concept.

"There are cultures in the world where people believe it is wrong to eat cows. This is true even if the people are poor and there is not adequate food for the children."

"So I've heard."

"Then you'll agree that this is clearly a different moral practice from ours. Only the most extreme animal-rights advocate in our society would condemn the killing of an animal if it were the only way to save human lives. So a society where killing cows is always wrong would appear to have different moral values from ours. There appears to be a greater respect for the lives of animals than for humans."

The middle-aged man and those around him were nodding in agreement. "So far, so good," he yelled out.

"But suppose we again ask our critical question: why did they carry out this practice? Suppose it is because they *believe* that after death the souls of humans inhabit the bodies of animals, especially cows. That cow just may be your grandmother."

Laughter spread through the room.

"Ah," said Ted, "you laugh, which tells us how different your belief about this particular piece of reality is from these people's."

Now they were nodding.

"But now, do we want to say that their values are different from ours? No. The difference lies elsewhere. It is in our *belief systems*, not in our values. We both agree we shouldn't eat Grandma. We simply disagree about whether the cow is or could be Grandma.

"So let me summarize here. We have said that different moral practices don't necessarily indicate a difference in moral values. They could result from different circumstances and conditions in life, or they could stem from different beliefs about reality."

The limitations of
the argument for
objective moral
standards

Without missing a beat, the young athletic man was on his feet again. "Does this mean, then," he asked, "that there are *no* differences in moral values anywhere in the world? Are you saying you have proven that?"

"Now that would be saying more than I could prove," answered Ted. "I don't need to tell you that I'm not omniscient. You see, the only way anyone could make that sweeping claim would be to have studied every cultural practice different from ours in the world. No one has done that."

"So you can't be sure," interrupted the young man, "that there are no differences in moral values somewhere in the world?"

"That is correct. Certainty is one thing I don't have. However, here is what we *can* say. In order for anyone to prove that different moral values exist between us and another group of people, they have to meet three conditions.

"First, they must find a moral practice that is *genuinely different* from ours. Second, they must show that this difference is not the result of different *beliefs* about reality. Third, they have to show that it is not the result of different *circumstances* and conditions of life either. Until these three conditions are met, no one can say there is a difference in moral values.

"And let me remind you of the major similarities in moral values among people. We see this in our daily conversations, and we saw it in the UN Declaration. Also recall the ancient moral codes. These are good reasons for believing that a single set of objective moral values exists and that all people recognize it, and that what appear to be differences in values can be accounted for as I have done."

When Ted had finished speaking, there was a brief silence. Most sat quietly, absorbing the wave of new ideas. The note-takers were busily getting them down.

But the silence didn't last long. Just as Ted thought the questions might be over, he heard rustling sounds to his left. Looking over, he saw the athletic-looking young man on his feet again with the same sheepish grin.

This time the audience erupted in spontaneous laughter. This was a tenacious young man, and they were beginning to like him.

Ted, also laughing, pointed toward him and said, "I see our chief spokesman on this issue has a supplementary question."

"Yes, I do. Just one more thing, if I may," said the young man courteously, somewhat embarrassed by all the attention.

"Of course."

"You have shown us quite convincingly," he began, "that the similarities in moral values are much greater than the differences. You have also argued that in order to show a true difference in moral values we must meet the three conditions you've set out."

"Yes."

"But did you not also admit that there could be genuine differences in values somewhere? You did say, did you not, that no one had checked every culture and every practice different from ours?"

Ted nodded. He admired the questioner's obvious ability to grasp ideas quickly and to probe them for adequacy.

"But this would mean," the young man continued, "that anthropologists might someday find a group of people with genuinely different moral values from ours. In fact, maybe some have already and we just don't know about them."

"It is conceivable, yes," Ted responded.

"My question is, then, if we found such a difference, how would it fit with this objective moral standard you say exists?"

The young man sat down, but no one could be sure for how long.

"You have pressed very hard," Ted replied. "Let's assume for purposes of discussion here that you are right, that in our travels during the next year one of us actually finds a group of people with genuine differences in moral value from ours. We find people who really do commend a practice that we condemn, and it can't be explained through a difference in circumstances or beliefs about reality."

The young man signaled his agreement with this exercise.

"The question then is," Ted continued, "what this would tell us about the status of morality? Would this rule out a single objective moral standard?"

"It would seem so," the young man spoke up, emboldened by his public exposure.

"But we must tread carefully here," Ted cautioned, raising his arm. "Some argue that it does, and their argument is sometimes called the 'cultural differences argument.'[6] It argues from a set of facts to a conclusion about the nature of morality."

"It does what? You just lost me there," interrupted the young man."

What moral practices tell us about morality

"Let me put it this way," Ted responded. "It starts by stating that different cultures have different values. That is an assertion of a particular fact. It then concludes from this assertion that there is therefore no objective truth in morality.

"Do you see how this argument moves from an assertion about the way things are to a conclusion about the status of morality?" he asked the young man.

The questioner and others nodded slowly.

"In essence, it is saying that because different cultures have different values, there can be no one objectively correct set of values. But what are we to say about this kind of argument?" Ted asked.

The audience was silent. Then an elderly woman near the front spoke up softly. "It seems okay to me. I mean, if different people hold different values, what else can we conclude?"

Some nodded their agreement. Others, however, looked doubtful about the argument.

"We must proceed carefully here," Ted cautioned. "There are two ways to critique this kind of argument. The first way is to question the truth of the assertion itself. We should ask if it really is true that different cultures have fundamentally different moral values from others. If not, the argument can't get started. No conclusion follows from the assertion if it is not true. And as a matter of fact, we've already seen that it is pretty doubtful. The outstanding feature of moral values around the world is the fundamental similarities among them, not the differences. And the differences that we do find can often be explained by a difference in a society's circumstances or in its beliefs about reality.

"You'll recall we've said all that, but I just want us to see that the very assertion on which the argument is founded is itself doubtful."

"So far I'm with you," nodded the young man, "but you said there were two ways to critique an argument like this."

"Yes. The second way is to ask whether the argument is logically valid. So let's do that. Let's assume, for purposes of argument, that you or I do find a group of people with genuinely different moral values from ours or from some other group's. How does the cultural differences argument go from here? It would conclude from this fact that there cannot be one single objective moral standard that all people know about. Our question is whether that conclusion follows logically from the fact, or premise, as we call it in logic. If it does, and if we do in fact find a group like this, then it will have been proved that no single objective moral standard exists. But does it follow?"

"I think it does!" spoke up the same elderly woman near the front. "How could an objective moral standard exist if we found a difference in moral values among people?"

"We know her opinion," joked Ted. "But I must say that here is where we must be very rigorous in our logic. You see, unfortunately, from a logical point of view that is not a valid argument. The conclusion does not really follow from the fact, which we call the premise. That is, even if the premise is true, the conclusion still might be false."

"But why?" asked the woman. "How can you be so sure?"

"Let me explain, and I think you'll agree. You see, the premise concerns what people *believe*. It says that in some societies people believe one thing is morally right; in others, people believe the same thing is not right. In other words, their beliefs differ.

"The conclusion, however, concerns what really is the case.

What disagreement tells us about morality

It states that because this disagreement exists, we can conclude that a single objective moral standard does not exist. But this is mistaken. The mere fact that people disagree about something does not tell us that there is no right or wrong viewpoint.

"Let me illustrate. Suppose we found a group of people who believed it was perfectly acceptable to eat the dead and another group who believed this was immoral. Does it follow from the mere fact that they disagreed"—he stopped to let those words sink in—"that there is no objective truth in the matter?"

As he looked out, he could see many were trying to make a quick but thoughtful decision.

"No, it does not. For it could be that this practice is objectively right, or wrong for that matter, and that one or the other of them is simply mistaken."

The woman was signaling her agreement.

"There are those who believe the earth is flat. The rest of us disagree. Are we to conclude that strictly because there is disagreement, there is no correct answer to the question of the shape of the earth? Of course not. We would never draw such a conclusion, because we realize that in their beliefs about the world, some people might simply be wrong. There is no reason to think that if the world is round everyone must know it.

"Similarly, if two people disagree about some moral matter, it is conceivable that one could be wrong and the other right."[7]

There was a familiar rustling to Ted's left. Looking over, he saw the young man on his feet again. "Could I have just one more question?" he asked. "It'll be brief, I promise."

"Please. Go ahead."

The invalidity of the cultural differences argument "I just want to know precisely what you have proven about this cultural differences argument. It set out to prove that there cannot be a single objective moral standard. Have you proven the conclusion is false?" He sat down.

"I wish!" answered Ted.

"Well, what exactly have you proven then?"

"Excellent question. We have not actually proved that the conclusion is false. But what we have done," Ted said, raising his voice just a little, "is show that the argument which sets out to prove that there cannot be a single objective moral standard fails to prove anything of the sort. It is invalid."

"Which means?"

"It means that this argument gives us no reason to believe a single objective moral standard cannot exist. In other words, we have shown that even if differences in moral values exist among people, that would still not be a reason to believe that a single objective moral standard does not exist. This is important because in order to determine whether or not an idea is true, we need arguments in its support. The argument given for believing that there could be no single objective moral standard turns out to be fallacious. So it proves nothing. And remember, we have seen plenty of reasons for thinking such an objective standard does exist."

"I see," said the young man.

At this point the emcee stepped to the podium. "I see we could go on all evening, but all good things must end sooner or later. The good professor has given us a provocative evening. Let's thank him."

Applause rippled through the auditorium.

"Your questions have also been insightful, and we've had a couple of pretty good dust-ups. In my opinion that constitutes a good evening. From now on we'll all be careful about labeling anything as morally good or bad, won't we? Remember what we're assuming when we do. Professor Douglas has called us to be consistent with our assumptions. Good night."

Ted was shuffling his notes back into order when he noticed Graham and Francine coming toward him with a handful of friends in tow. "Why, hello!" he grinned. "Wasn't that some marathon?"

"Pure enjoyment!" returned Graham enthusiastically as most of the crowd left, including one man who returned to his large house to ponder the evening.

But Francine was not ready to leave yet. "Let's assume you're right," she spoke up, "about these objective moral standards."

"You mean I've convinced you that objective moral standards do exist?"

"Now I didn't say that!"

"No, I don't suppose I could have been that lucky."

"But I am willing to grant it for purposes of argument," she added quickly. "I do think, though, that if they do exist, they raise more questions than they answer."

"Hey!" Ted shot back. "I've been answering questions all evening! What more do you want? What's left?" By this time a small circle was pressing in on them to hear the postlecture discussion.

"Where do they come from?" asked Francine.

"Where do what come from?"

The question of the foundation of objective moral standards "These objective moral principles," Francine replied. "Let's face it. Agreeing that they exist is one thing; explaining their existence is quite another. I would like to know how you would explain their existence. How did they get here? Where do they come from?"

Others nodded their agreement.

"Uh-huh." Ted held up his hand. "I think I see what you're after. You're asking for the basis or ground of this objective moral truth. You're asking what accounts for the existence of moral principles that are binding and obligatory on us—even on the person who doesn't agree with them?"

"That's it!"

"A very good question. *Ex nihilo nihil fit.*"

"What? Now we're switching to Latin?" asked Graham.

"No. That's a very common phrase. It states a principle that seems to be embedded in the very framework of our thinking. We all assume it. None of us can escape it or even imagine thinking without it. The phrase means 'from nothing, nothing comes.' "

"Now I recall it from my first class in philosophy," mused Francine.

"Yes, and the very fact that you're seeking the basis or explanation for objective moral truth shows that you are acting on it. And that goes for all of you, even if you've never heard of it. If something exists, then your minds immediately begin searching for its cause. The idea that it could exist uncaused seems impossible to the human mind."

"Then you agree it's a good question," said Francine. "Now what's the answer?"

"As a matter of fact," Graham spoke up, "we atheists have an answer to that question."

Ted glanced at his watch. "Hey!" he cut in. "Before we get started, I'm afraid I'm a little tuckered out by now."

"What? You looked like you were having fun up there," said Francine.

"And I was, but you know what this mental strain can do to a person."

"Don't I!"

"I have a better suggestion," Ted went on.

"There you go placing moral value on your own suggestions," quipped someone in the circle.

"Oh, that word *better*. Don't get me sidetracked. Actually, I don't mean better morally, maybe better from a purely pragmatic standpoint."

"The suggestion . . . ?" asked Graham, moving his hand in a circle as if to pull it out of him.

"Yes. Don't we have another luncheon planned for us at the mystery house?"

"Yes!" exclaimed a jubilant Graham. "The mystery house. I nearly forgot. Do we know who the mystery host is yet?"

"Not unless you know something we don't," replied Ted. "Whoever heard of such an arrangement?"

"Someone's up to something," muttered Graham, "and someday we're going to find out who and what it is."

"Let's continue this discussion at the luncheon," suggested Francine.

They all nodded.

"And we'll hear an atheist answer to this question then."

"You're on," said Graham.

By this time the auditorium had emptied. The little circle dispersed.

Part 2
FOUNDATIONS OF OBJECTIVE MORAL STANDARDS

7
MORALS
WITHOUT GOD
An Atheist
Foundation

T ed arrived as usual and was greeted by the doorkeeper. They exchanged a few words on the way to
the reception room, and the doorkeeper told him he
was the first to arrive. "Help yourself to some coffee," the
doorkeeper said, and immediately left.

Alone in the room, Ted found a cup and coffee and took
a closer look at his surroundings. Although perfectly deco-
rated and furnished, the room lacked some of the personal
touches one might expect to see. There were no family
photographs, memorabilia or anything that might identify
the host. *How curious,* he mused, but his thoughts were
diverted by the arrival of the others.

First was William, the visiting scholar who had so openly
announced his evolutionary convictions the other evening.
"Hello, Ted!" he exclaimed cheerily. "I heard you gave a

stimulating lecture the other evening. It was on"—he paused momentarily to check his pocket calendar—"yes, the existence of objective moral standards."

"You keep accurate records," Ted quipped.

"And I expect our discussion today will focus on something similar."

"I expect you're right," Ted said. "Oh look, here's Ian. Why hello, Ian! You still feel it's worth your time to come to these lunches?"

"Oh," responded Ian, "given that I'm a humanist, the basis of morals has always interested me greatly. Just last year our Humanist Society asked me to research the best ways of laying a humanistic foundation for morality."

"You mean . . . ?" Graham was dumbfounded.

"Yes!" responded Ian. "I've researched this issue before."

Ted shook his head. He thought back to that first day when they all met at the big house and wondered why they were there. Could it be a coincidence that Ian had researched the very question that was beginning to dominate their conversations? *What are the chances of that?* he thought.

He was interrupted by the sound of Ian's voice. "Isn't an atheistic foundation for morals being presented here today?"

Just then Graham and Francine strode in. "Yes, it is!" Graham announced, overhearing the question.

"This should be good," Ian returned. "I've always been interested in how you atheists do that."

"Hey!" Graham shot back. "I'm aware that many people cannot imagine what foundation an atheist could have. Once God is gone, moral foundations disappear too, or so they think."

"And I take it you don't agree?" asked Ted.

"The man's a genius," quipped Graham.

The impossibility of uncaused objective moral standards

Just then William walked over with a tray of cups full of hot, steaming brew for the newcomers.

"Ah, the smell of fresh coffee!" smiled Ted, taking a deep

breath. "In one sense it's just like objective moral value, isn't it?"

"Coffee, like objective moral value?" asked Francine, looking a bit doubtful. "Am I missing something, or have you been in the ivory tower too long? What similarity do you see between objective moral value and coffee?"

"Well, think of it this way. When you smell that fresh aroma, doesn't your mind immediately assume there must be something else causing it?"

"Uh-huh, but . . ."

"And it's something you may or may not see? A different entity altogether?"

"Yes, of course. There must be coffee somewhere nearby, causing the aroma that we are enjoying."

"Precisely," responded Ted. "So we could say, 'Where there's a coffee aroma, there's coffee.' "

"Sure. Just like we say, 'Where there's smoke, there's fire.' "

"Making up your own examples—that's good! Have you considered a career in teaching?"

"Well, I didn't actually make it up."

"No, but you did recall it and use it correctly, which shows you understand the point."

"And what is the point?"

"The point," stated Ted, "is the same one I made last night after the lecture. Remember, *ex nihilo nihil fit.*"

"Yes, yes. From nothing, nothing comes."

"You've just stated the principle of causality. It's a principle we apply to everything we experience."

"Principle of what?" Francine pressed.

"Causality. Isn't it true," Ted continued, "that whenever anything comes into existence, we automatically assume there is a cause for it somewhere?"

"I guess I'd have to think about that one," mused Francine.

"Probably not too long. Few have been willing to deny it. Doing so means you have to believe that something popped into existence completely uncaused, out of nothing."[1]

Ted went on. "Sometimes the causes of things are obvious and simple."

"Like this coffee aroma." Francine held up her cup.

"Right. Other times they're more difficult, and because knowing them is not important to us, we don't feel the need to discover them."

"Such as?"

"Take the force of gravity. We all know it's there, but most of us just don't feel enough need to know its cause to inquire into it. But," he continued, "there are also certain causes of things which are more difficult to discover, yet it is important to us to know them."

"An example?" Francine leaned forward, putting her fingertips together.

"Objective moral value!" Ted laughed.

"I should have known. There had to be a connection somewhere. So both objective moral value and this coffee aroma exist and are caused by something else we may or may not be able to see."

"Precisely. The difference, of course, is that the cause of objective moral value is more difficult to discover."

"Perhaps that's why many people don't try to find it at all," remarked Francine. "At least that's my experience."

"That's probably part of it," replied Ted, "but obviously you aren't stopped by that. That was your question last night after the lecture. It's too important to ignore."

"But what makes it so important?" spoke up William. "Why should we inquire into this particular cause?"

The importance of finding the cause

There was an abrupt silence. Then Graham spoke up. "Here's why," he said. "In fact, there are at least two reasons. First, because of the immense influence that it has over human conduct. Not only does objective moral value powerfully affect our own decisions, views and actions. It also affects the way we feel about the actions of others. Because we believe certain things are objectively right or wrong, we feel justified in condemning or commending certain actions of other people. If we didn't believe that, we would not feel so justified. My point is, anything that exerts that much influence over our conduct is worth understanding as fully as we can."

"But you said there were two reasons," pressed William.

"Yes, I did. The second is that its cause also must be highly influential. I'm speaking of the entity standing behind objective moral value. I would say it this way: anything that causes something this influential in human conduct, as we've seen objective value to be, must also be worth knowing about. Whatever this cause is, it is exerting a great amount of influence over your life and mine."

They all got comfortable in their chairs and settled in for a good discussion.

"So how do we discover its cause?" asked Francine, leaning forward with interest.

"Various answers have been given to that question," answered Ted. "I suggest we look at some of the better-known ones to see if the answer lies with any of them. That would only be proper methodology."

"Right. You philosophers are big on things like methodology and procedure."

"It does help us get to the bottom of an issue. I imagine that in the world of business, politics or what have you, there must be procedures and methods to help you achieve your goals."

"I guess so—when you put it like that."

"But let's not get sidetracked. Method is only a tool to help us work through a question properly."

"Okay, our question then is—?" asked Francine.

"Let's clarify it," exclaimed Ted. "Our question is: how do we explain the existence of objective moral value? How do we account for it? How did it get here?"

"Oh, like the coffee aroma, or the smoke."

"Exactly. And here is where we turn to you, Graham. You're an atheist, and you've got an atheistic foundation for objective morals."

"Yes, I do," responded a confident Graham. "As I see it, it's really quite simple."

"Well, now, there's a point in its favor," said Francine.

"And I think you'll see others as well."

"We'll be the judge of that," she retorted.

The atheist's starting point: moral truisms

"Of course. Now for the justification." He began rolling up his sleeves. "You begin with certain moral truisms." He spoke slowly so as to say it precisely. This academic discussion was proving to be quite a mind-stretcher.

"I'm afraid that's a new term to me," said Ian.

"Oh, I just mean rather simple moral statements which most would accept as obviously true. Statements like suffering is bad, keeping promises is good, truth is something to be valued, racial discrimination is immoral. Most everyone accepts these as true. I call them moral truisms. To justify them, you organize them into a coherent package." He drew his hands in a large circle.

Justification by coherence

"You mean they all must fit together, agree with one another," Francine interjected.

"Exactly!" Graham replied.

"Sounds reasonable."

"Of course. But furthermore, they also must fit together with everything else we know about the world, society and human nature. We must arrange all the elements into wide reflective equilibrium."

"Wide reflective what?" Francine asked incredulously.

"Equilibrium," Graham laughed. "That just means all the moral truisms and other ideas about the world must work together as a coherent system. But here's the important part. That coherence itself provides the justification of the truisms. If we have a system that works—no part conflicts with any other part—then that system has a certain justification. The coherence itself justifies it. We need no other justification for it.[2]

"There you have it," he said confidently. "As you can all see, there is no need to appeal to God to provide a foundation for morality." He leaned back and sipped his coffee.

"That's it?" queried Ted, both hands open.

"You sound as if I need more."

"Maybe you do, but we'll find that out by asking what we all think of this explanation."

"It sounds like a novel idea to me," spoke up Francine.

"Actually, it's quite commonly known among those who study ethical theory," replied Graham.

"It's true," added Ted. "Graham is in the company of some respected thinkers."

"That's a comforting thought," Graham mused wryly.

"Of course," Ted continued, "that in itself doesn't make it a good foundation."

"Hey! It can't hurt either."

"Right. It neither helps nor hurts. The fact that someone does or does not believe an idea never makes that idea true or false. Ideas must be proven on their own merit. So let's get back to the important question. Does Graham's atheist foundation succeed or not? And let's remember what it will have to do to succeed. It will have to adequately account for the existence of objective moral value."

"I like it!" replied Ian enthusiastically. "It's straightforward and simple. And isn't coherence a sign of correctness in anything?"

"Whoa there a minute!" Ted cut in. "Are you sure about that?"

"What's the problem?" Ian persisted. "Surely coherence is a good and necessary quality. Every set of ideas must be coherent if it's going to be true. And we know for sure that incoherence is a sign of incorrectness. If a set of ideas contains contradictions, if any idea conflicts with any other, then the whole set must be rejected. Isn't that so?" *The limits of the value of coherence*

"Now *that* is correct," replied Ted. "Incoherence proves incorrectness, but that is different from what you said first. Didn't you say that coherence proves correctness?"

Ian nodded.

"Well, that's a very different point. Here is an important distinction. Any true set of ideas must be coherent. That we *The inability of coherence alone to prove truth* know. But we cannot also say that any coherent set of ideas must be true. We could say it this way: although a true set of ideas must be coherent, a coherent set of ideas need not necessarily be true. Coherence, alone, does not prove truth."

All were listening intently, aware of the importance of this distinction.

"Think of it this way," Ted continued. "Would it not be possible to construct a set of ideas—a viewpoint, shall we say—which is clearly mistaken and yet consists of ideas that agree with one another? These ideas could all be wrong in just such a way that they agree with each other. This set of ideas would be coherent, yet untrue."

At this Graham leaned forward. "Okay, so it's possible to have coherence without truth. But you still haven't shown me that the coherent set of moral truisms I could construct is false."

"No, I haven't," agreed Ted. "For all we know, you could construct one that is true. In fact, a true set of moral ideas must be coherent. As we said, incoherence would disprove any system of ideas."

"Well then?"

"What I have shown is that you need something more than coherence alone to show your ideas are true. Coherence by itself will never do it, as you earlier claimed. It can never act as an adequate reason that anyone else ought to believe your ideas are true. Isn't that what you were arguing?"

"Hmm." Graham thought quietly for a moment and then said, "So my ideas may be true, but coherence alone does not prove they are true."

"Exactly! It does not provide an adequate foundation for any moral system."

The group was momentarily quiet.

"Would anyone like lunch?" Ian's question was a welcome diversion from the intensity of the moment.

"Ooh, I can't resist that sight!" spoke up Francine. "That buffet is calling me "

"Oh, please!" Graham sputtered.

They filled their plates and agreed that someone was going to a considerable effort to satisfy their appetites. They sat and munched for a while, but it wasn't long before the discussion began again.

"You seem to have weakened my justification for objective morals," Graham said to Ted.

"And I've only given one of the problems with it," Ted replied.

"You mean there's more?"

"Actually, the second is more an extension of the first. You see, you have used coherence as a way of justifying objective moral standards."

"Right."

"But since, as we've seen, coherence is not a proof of the truth of a set of ideas, a potential problem always lurks in the background."

"And what might that be?"

"Conflicting moral viewpoints."

"By which you mean what?" Graham was less than enthused with the entrance of this new idea.

"Ask yourself," responded Ted. "Is it not at least *possible* to have two or more coherent moral systems or viewpoints that conflict with one another? Each coherent within itself, functioning well as an individual unit, and yet conflicting with other equally coherent viewpoints. One commending what another condemns. Surely that is at least possible." *The implications of coherent yet conflicting moral viewpoints*

Graham grew very thoughtful. He had to admit this seemed at least possible. "Do you have an example?"

Ted leaned forward, folding his hands on the table. "Think of the Nazi atrocities inflicted upon Jews under Adolf Hitler," he said very seriously. "Brutalities almost beyond belief. How did so many bring themselves to carry out such heinous actions?"

"Good question," mused Graham. "I've wondered about that."

"They did it," continued Ted, "by convincing themselves *What the Nazis teach us* that a certain idea was true: namely, that the Jewish race was somehow inferior to the rest of us. They were subhuman. Once they became convinced of that, an entirely new moral system or viewpoint was allowed to emerge—and a coherent one at that. The rules about how humans ought to be treated need not apply to Jews any longer, because they were beneath the rest of us in dignity, value and importance. Killing them en masse, or using them for torturous experiments for the benefit of the rest of us, became perfectly justified."

"But that's absurd! It's nonsense! It's . . ." Graham slammed his cup down on the table.

"The point is not whether you or I agree with this moral viewpoint. It is not even whether the Germans all did. And, in fact, many German people of the time did not. But that is not the relevant issue."

"Well, then, what is?" Graham was growing impatient.

"You should know," replied Ted. "You established it for us. The only issue here is whether this moral system is coherent. Remember, you said that if a moral system is coherent, then it is justified as an objectively true moral system."

Graham protested. "But I would argue that this moral system is not coherent. I mean, it seems arbitrary and incoherent to simply exclude a group of human beings and call them inferior. Isn't that inconsistent? If they are humans like the rest of us, shouldn't the moral rules applied to humans apply to them all?"

"That argument may be worth a try, but in the end it will be pointless," answered Ted. "You see, it is true that humans all have some basic traits in common. We all have rational, moral, sensory, nutritional and reproductive capacities, to name a few. However, it is also true that we are not all identical. There are differences in intellectual capacity, skin color, gender, athletic ability and other areas."

"But these features aren't important!" Graham was adamant.

"Actually, the question about precisely which features or qualities give something rights to decent treatment is continually debated. Philosopher Peter Singer and others argue that this 'rights-giving feature' is the ability to feel pain and pleasure. This would mean, of course, that animals would then have the same rights to equal treatment as humans have, which is precisely what Singer argues. You see, even though animals are unlike humans in some ways, they can and do feel pain and pleasure much as humans do, and this, says Singer, is the relevant similarity."[3]

Animal research and experimentation had long been a pet peeve of Graham's, and he had read Singer's arguments. "Yes, I've studied Singer," he commented. "And I agree with him."

"But others don't," rejoined Ted. "They argue that it is the capacity to reason that gives these important rights. This would exclude animals and include only humans.[4]

"Still others argue it is the characteristic of being a teleological center of life that gives a being special rights."

"A what?" Francine asked, totally nonplused.

"That just refers to any being that has the ability to pursue its own goals in its own way in the widest sense. But notice, this would include all living things, humans, animals and, yes, even plants. And in case you're wondering, yes, this is a view held by some philosophers. It is used to argue that humans and animals are not, by their very nature, superior to plants. Plants too are able to pursue their own ends in their own way."[5]

"Whew! Isn't that a little extreme?"

"It may be, but let's not miss the point here. All these viewpoints are coherent, yet they conflict with each other. For Hitler to go one step further and select some other feature that would apply to all humans except Jews would be equally coherent. He could merely find something in the Jewish race that is not present in others, even if it were just the fact that they are Jews, with all that entails of their history and culture."

"I would argue with him that he has chosen the wrong feature," Graham persisted.

"But you can't. Not so long as coherence is our criterion. Remember, we may think it's the wrong feature. We may consider the choice of it to be groundless and arbitrary, but it is coherent. It is not self-contradictory, and that's all your theory requires."

Graham looked frustrated.

"Here, then, is the critical question. Suppose we adopt coherence as the criterion for justification of objective moral value. What then can we say to Hitler or anyone else who gains sufficient power to actually implement his moral system? If it is coherent, it passes our test and is therefore as justified as your or my moral system."

They were all silent for a moment. Then Graham spoke. "So we can't condemn Hitler. That's a bitter pill."

The inability to judge between coherent yet conflicting viewpoints

"Correct," Ted said wryly. "Furthermore, so long as coherence is the only criterion for justifying our moral statements, we have no way to judge between any two or more conflicting moral viewpoints so long as each is coherent. And we've seen that can happen quite easily."

"I have to give you that," responded Graham quietly.

"So if a person comes to you with a moral viewpoint that conflicts with yours and you find both are coherent, you are left with no way to determine which is superior. And this is true regardless of how abhorrent the viewpoint may be. But realize that if two ideas or viewpoints conflict, at least one must be wrong. They simply cannot both be right. That would violate one of the most fundamental laws of logic, the law of noncontradiction. But the coherence criterion gives no way of judging between them."

"But we do distinguish between better and worse moral viewpoints," replied Graham, extending both hands for emphasis. "Hitler's morality was worse than Mother Teresa's. There—I just did it."

"Yes, we do. But when we do, we aren't using the coherence criterion anymore for this distinction. So long as Mother Teresa's and Adolf Hitler's viewpoints are both coherent, the coherence criterion judges them to be equally good. Any distinctions you make are coming from some other criterion lurking in the back of your mind."

Graham became very thoughtful. A solemn quietness settled over the group. Hard ideas, these. As much as he disliked it, Graham was beginning to lose confidence in his own method of justifying objective moral truth.

A plate of irresistible pastries was passed around to go with a last cup of coffee, but the thought process continued unabated.

"Before we leave this issue," said Ted, "I must point out one more difficulty with it."

"You mean there's still more?" Graham was incredulous.

"Afraid so. This one is perhaps the most basic of all, and quite simple really. You see, you said earlier that to justify objective moral value, we simply begin with moral truisms, these widely accepted moral statements, and then construct them into a coherent package."

"Right."

"Well, you have to ask yourself what actually is being gained when you do this. Remember, we are looking for an adequate explanation for the objective moral standards we all know about. That was what got us into this whole inquiry. But that is just to say we're looking for an explanation for these very moral truisms. Their existence is precisely the problem we are dealing with. Why are there such things as moral truisms? Why are there basic moral ideas about which most of us instinctively agree and hold to be true regardless of what others may think? To simply begin with them begs the question of how they exist, which is what we are asking."

Moral truisms: not the place to begin

Graham thought hard. "Are you telling me that the coherence criterion is really no justification at all?"

"Afraid so. Using moral truisms as your starting point is entirely different from explaining their existence. It ignores the critical question—namely, how is their existence explained?"

"Well, that does it!" said an exasperated Graham. "I knew I shouldn't have gotten into this with all of you. A sure-fire recipe for losing an argument!"

"Hey, wait a minute!" exclaimed Ted. "I thought we were looking for truth here. We're not playing games of winning or losing. If we move closer to the truth, then the way I see it we're all winners."

"It's still not easy, discarding one's views."

Discarding views: a part of learning "Actually, it's a part of learning. You might say it comes with the territory. We all have to do it at one time or another. In fact, people who refuse to change their minds seriously limit their chances of learning."

Graham was not amused, but he fell silent. Then he muttered, barely audibly, "So the coherence model doesn't adequately explain the existence of objective moral truth."

Ted nodded his agreement. Graham muttered something unpleasant to himself.

"Well, then, what does?" piped up Francine, bolting forward in her chair.

"Ah! Major question," replied Ted.

"Which I would like to answer," interrupted Ian.

"But you're a secular humanist!" cut in William.

"That's right, I am. So what's the problem?"

"And you are going to provide a foundation for objective moral standards?"

"Yes. Surely you don't believe that we secular humanists cannot be good moral people simply because we are humanists!"

"Well, well. A secular humanist foundation for morals. This should be good. But"—William glanced at his watch— "it will have to wait for our next get-together. How time flies when one discusses moral judgments."

They all went their separate ways in the transportation provided. A rest from the mental overload would be welcome, but already they couldn't help but wonder what Ian's foundation would be like.

8
CAN WE BE THE BASIS OF MORALS?
A Humanist Foundation, Part I

The luncheons were becoming a regular part of Ted's life and were duly marked on his calendar. The following week, the pattern was repeated again. As he hopped out of the car, he thought about the mystery host, the unseen cause of their coming together, and was determined to find out more. He asked the doorkeeper, "Can you tell me anything about our host or why we are here?"

The doorkeeper pondered the question as they walked across the foyer. Then he spoke. "The time will soon come when you will find out. I assure you there is a good reason for these meetings. If you continue to come, all will be explained eventually. Please enjoy your stay this afternoon."

Ted entered the room to find his friends. After brief greetings, they quickly forgot other concerns, and their thoughts returned to their last conversation.

"I've been thinking," spoke up Ian, looking at Graham, "about your comment on changing our minds. I'm wondering why you say it's so hard."

"That's easy for you to say," Graham shot back. "It's not your view that's being challenged."

"He has a point," agreed Ted.

"Well, with all due respect," said Ian, looking toward Graham, "I have to admit I never did think too highly of your coherence explanation, right from the moment you mentioned it. There seems to me to be a better way to account for objective moral standards."

"Yes, you told us so last week. So what *would* a secular humanist have to say about the basis for objective moral value?"

"What do you mean, *secular* humanist?" Francine interrupted. "Aren't all humanists secular?"

Two types of humanists: secular and Christian

"Actually, no," Ted cut in. "There is at least one group that is not. Christian humanists."

"That sounds like an oxymoron to me."

"Only if you can't be a Christian and a humanist at the same time. But Christian humanists believe they can."

"You're a Christian," Francine continued. "Don't tell me you're also claiming to be a humanist?"

"As a matter of fact, I am. But Christian humanism is very different from the kind of humanism most people think of when they hear the word—so much so that some Christians are reluctant even to use the term *humanist* to describe themselves."

"And you're not?"

"Not at all. In fact, in my view only Christian humanism provides an adequate basis for the value and dignity of humans, which is so important to all humanists. Christian humanism teaches that humans are the highest and most valuable of all God's creation. Because we are made in God's image, we humans have certain abilities no other created things have. We can create, love, assert, reflect on our past and future, and so forth. This gives humans an intrinsic dignity beyond that of animals.

"Furthermore, according to the Christian humanist, we ought to develop our human potential as fully as possible, always remembering our position under God. We even have our own Christian humanist manifesto."[1]

"Whatever Ted's view is," responded Ian, "I call myself a secular humanist to distinguish myself from any religious viewpoint whatsoever. Religion and God are irrelevant to my life and views. Human beings are the measure of all things. There is nothing greater or more significant than us humans."

"So back to my question," said Graham. "What would a secular humanist have to say about the foundation of objective moral standards?"

"Just the invitation I was looking for," Ian quipped. "As a matter of fact, this issue has always interested me greatly. I'm well aware that many people find it surprising that a secular humanist could have any foundation for moral principles."

"And I take it you're saying you do," responded Ted.

"Yes, and a very adequate one at that," Ian replied confidently.

"Now that is what we'll have to see," said Ted. "And, of course, we'll only know once we've subjected your moral foundation to proper scrutiny."

Ian leaned forward on the edge of his seat and moved his coffee cup aside to make room for the habitual hand gestures which were sure to come. "If we were calling Graham's explanation the coherence model, I'll call mine the human nature model."

Graham was intrigued. "The what model?"

"Human nature. It seems to me that objective moral values really do exist and are rooted in our human nature. They are our guide as to which actions are good and evil."

Human nature: the foundation of morality

"I hope you'll explain this!" Graham pressed.

"Of course. If objective moral value is rooted in human nature, it would mean that if an action violates human nature, it is wrong. If it does not, it is morally good or at least neutral. Don't you see? This would explain why there would be agreement on certain basic moral ideas even in different times and places. Even though the time and place may be different, human nature remains constant, unchanging in its essence. Being a human today means the same as it did a few hundred years ago. The same acts that violate human nature in one time and place do so in another."

William's face lit up. "Fascinating! Do you have an example?"

Ian thought for a moment. "Slavery," he said. "Wouldn't we all agree that to treat human beings as though they were property is to violate their natures?"

"I guess so," responded William, "but what exactly do you mean by someone's nature?"

"A person's nature is what he or she is. To ask what human nature is is to ask what it means to be a human. Humans by nature are beings that are rational, social, moral and free, among other things. Is that not correct?"

"Uh-huh."

"Which means we humans have the abilities to think, remember, initiate activity, make decisions, plan ahead and live according to our own plans, just to name a few."

"So you agree with Christian humanism?"

What it means to violate someone's nature "In that way, sure. The difference is we secular humanists explain all this without reference to God or religion. But back to my point. By violating someone's nature, I mean treating people as though they are something they are not, usually as something lower and less valuable. It usually means not permitting people to express their uniquely human abilities. That ignores the dignity, value and respect human beings deserve because of the kind of beings we are."

"And you are saying," William pressed, "that slavery is

wrong precisely because it does this to human beings?"

"Exactly. Slavery ignores the essence of human nature. It neglects the fact that all human beings are rational, social, moral and free. It treats some people as if they were on a level similar to animals—of the same value, worth or dignity as animals. Owning humans or using them as laboring animals is wrong precisely because it violates their nature. That lifestyle does not fit with the capacities or abilities of a human being. It would hinder or squelch the full development of human capacities."[2]

William sat forward. "Well stated, Ian! Now let's ask what we think of this proposal. Does it adequately account for the existence of objective moral value?"

"I'm impressed!" Francine responded. "This sounds abundantly adequate to me."

"Thank you!" joked Ian. "I'll register your support."

"Now that sounds like the politician in him." Francine smiled. Anyone who knew Ian at all was aware that he not only was an activist in the local humanist club but also had bigger political ambitions. For a moment his mind turned to the decision he knew he would have to make sooner or later: which party to identify with for the long term. Social and moral issues played most heavily on his mind, and he hoped the current discussions would guide him in these choices.

The sound of Ted's voice jerked him back to present reality. "I can see you are quite taken with this human nature model," he was saying to Francine. "Just what do you find so appealing in it?"

"For one thing, it's straightforward and simple," she replied.

"Yeah—that's what she said about my explanation, if you'll recall," complained Graham.

"Yes, I did. But this model also seems to avoid some of the problems we discovered in your coherence model."

"Such as?"

"Well, for one thing, this model doesn't just start with

moral truisms and assume they are true as you did. The human nature model tells *why* certain acts are wrong—because they violate human nature."

"She's right," interjected Ted. "A distinct advantage over the coherence model."

"And that one leads us to another," added Ian. "Because my model tells us *why* certain actions are wrong, it also gives us a basis for condemning them, however coherent they may be, and for commending others. Remember, we couldn't do that on the coherence model. So long as two viewpoints were coherent, they had to be judged of equal value. On my model, if an action violates human nature, it is wrong and worse than one that does not, and that's that regardless of its coherence or other merits."

"Quite insightful, I must say," responded Ted. "However, in your zeal to compare your model with the last one, you have overlooked one other problem with the coherence model."

"Which?"

"Our first one. If you'll recall, we agreed that coherence alone does not prove truth. It is at least possible for a viewpoint to consist of ideas that cohere with one another and still be wrong."

"Sure, I recall that. Why bring it up here?"

"Because I take it you would welcome the same kind of examination of your human nature model as we gave to Graham's coherence model?"

Ian was brimming with confidence. "Of course. I have nothing to hide!"

"Listen to him," intoned Graham.

Ted continued. "Then we must ask the same questions of it."

"That sounds fair, but I'm not clear on what questions you're getting at."

Ted leaned forward, motioning the others to come closer to him. As they did, he began softly. "We have seen that coherence alone is not sufficient to prove a moral viewpoint correct."

They all nodded.

"Now then, we must ask whether violating human nature alone is sufficient to make a moral viewpoint incorrect. And if so, why."

There was silence for a moment.

"You see," he continued, "that is the whole basis for the human nature model. Whereas the coherence model began by simply accepting moral truisms as true, the human nature model begins by simply accepting the idea that violating human nature is wrong."

The unstated assumption of the human nature model

"Well, isn't it?" Ian was adamant.

"It may be, but we must realize precisely what we are doing when we begin this way. We are assuming something we have not proved—namely, that if something violates human nature, it is for that reason immoral. But what will we say to the person who disagrees with that assumption? And remember, an assumption it is."

Ian was somewhat taken aback. "But that would be incredible!"

"Maybe so, to you and me. But what one person finds incredible another sees as perfectly acceptable. That is nothing more than a personal reaction. It can vary from person to person. It tells us nothing about the truth of an idea that someone may find incredible.

"Let's also remember that some have constructed moral viewpoints that do in fact disregard your assumption. The fact that their actions have violated human nature has not been a problem to *them*. Now what will we say to a person who holds such a viewpoint and gains sufficient power to implement it?"

"You mean like an Adolf Hitler?" Ian bristled at the thought that Hitler's actions could not be condemned on his model.

"Right. Hitler carried out many actions that treated Jews, Gypsies and others like property. What's more, he convinced many of his countrymen that these actions were justified. Obviously, the fact that they violated human nature was not a problem to him or them. And there have been others: Idi Amin, Joseph Stalin, Nero—and, for that matter, others like them who never gained power or became famous. My point is that viewpoints like this have been constructed. How will we show them they are wrong?"

"My point is," interrupted Graham, "I'm starving! Let's show them they're wrong after we eat!"

The others laughed, and the tension of the discussion was eased. As they made their way to the table, Ian was especially thankful for the interruption, because he had to admit he had no answer to this question.

After their appetite for food had been satisfied, their appetite for interaction was renewed, and Ted continued. "As a matter of fact, Ian, there are two ways someone could go about arguing that your assumption about human nature is not merely unproven but actually unfounded and mistaken."

"You mean my assumption that acts violating human nature are wrong?"

"Yes."

"How would anyone argue such a thing?" Ian was visibly defensive.

"Let me put the first problem with it to you this way: why us?"

"I'm afraid I don't follow."

The arbitrariness of choosing human nature as the moral foundation

"Don't you see, you've selected *human* nature as that which, if an act violates it, the act is wrong. But why human nature? What makes us so special, so worthy of being the one species in which morality is rooted?"

"I think there's a perfectly good reason for choosing humans," replied Ian. "It is because humans have certain abilities and capacities that other things—say plants, animals and rocks—don't have. Humans are a higher level of life. We have much greater capacity for reason, for creativity and for other activities than other beings. Therefore it stands to reason that human nature, and not animal nature or any other nature, ought to be the root of objective morality."

"That's a good try, Ian," responded Ted, "but I'm afraid it will only lead us back one step."

"How so?"

"You have chosen humans because they have a higher capacity for reason, creativity and the like than animals and other beings."

"Right."

"But suppose we ask why you have selected these particular abilities. Why reason and creativity? What makes these so important that the beings who possess them in the highest degree must be the root of objective morality? Why not choose powers of sense perception like sight, smell, hearing? In possession of these qualities, many animals are superior to humans."

Ted continued, "One could almost say: how convenient. You have chosen just those qualities that include *your* species and exclude others. This looks like the ultimate in arbitrary, preferential treatment. It goes beyond racism and sexism. It's what some call speciesism."

"Speciesism?"

"Yes. Didn't you say, Graham, that you had read some of philosopher Peter Singer's writings? Singer uses that word to describe—actually to condemn—the very kind of practice Ian seems to be advocating: giving preferential treatment to members of our own species, and mistreating or neglecting other species for no other reason than that they are different species that do not have the particular qualities we have.[3]

"My point, Ian, is that your human nature model gives no reason why human nature should be the chosen nature— if you violate it, a wrong is done. That is your most fundamental assumption. Your entire model rests on it."

A quietness settled over the table, but Ian was the quietest of all.

Ted broke the silence. "But you'll recall I said there were *two* arguments we could advance against the assumption that violating human nature is wrong."

"That's right—there's more, isn't there?" Ian's lack of excitement was apparent to all.

"It's not quite as inspiring when the shoe's on the other foot, is it?" remarked Graham.

Ian glared back but said nothing.

"But isn't there more coffee? I'm overdue for a second cup."

Even Ian chuckled and held his cup aloft to be refilled by Graham, who had gotten the coffeepot. After stirring his coffee, Ian said, "Okay, Ted, let's hear it."

"Yes. The second difficulty with your assumption that violating human nature is wrong is a logical one," announced Ted.

The problem with deriving moral claims from facts alone "It is known to philosophers as the fact-value problem. Or some call it the is-ought problem. It's actually a distinction made by philosophers. The philosopher David Hume is well known for articulating it."[4]

"It sounds foreign to me," Ian responded. "We humanists try to work with hard facts. This sounds mighty theoretical."

"Actually," answered Ted, "this distinction isn't that difficult, and I think you'll see you can't avoid it any more than we can when you do ethics, which you do. Your humanist views have ethical implications too."

"I won't deny that," Ian responded. "So what's this distinction?"

"Follow me carefully here," invited Ted, again leaning forward and motioning the others to move closer. "I may have to challenge an idea that is almost universally accepted. You see, many people act as if they can go directly from a purely factual statement to a value judgment."

"Stop right there!" exclaimed Ian. "What do you mean, factual and value statements?"

The meaning of factual statements "Let me put it this way," replied Ted. "This distinction simply recognizes two kinds of statements. The first kind we call purely factual statements, such as 'The sky is blue' or 'There are five of us here.' These statements make factual assertions, nothing more. They merely assert that something is the case."

"I'm with you so far."

"The second kind consists of value judgments, such as *The meaning of* 'We ought not to be here' or 'It is wrong to tell a lie.' These *moral judgments* statements go further and state that something ought to be the case. Statements like these we call value judgments.

"The point in all of this is that these two kinds of state- *The logical gap* ments are fundamentally different. There is a logical gap *between facts and* between the two, and we can't move from one to the other *values* without an adequate stepping stone, something to bridge that gap. We could call this a bridge premise."

"That sounds obvious enough," replied Ian.

"But it's often overlooked. As a matter of fact, this move from one to the other is very commonly made without a stepping stone."

"I'm not sure about the rest here, but this is all new to me," Ian continued. "Tell me more. How exactly do we make this wrong step from facts to values?"

Ted thought for a minute and then said, "I once read of a man who was told he ought to donate bone marrow to his sick cousin. When he asked why, he was told that if he didn't, his cousin would die."

"So what's wrong with that?" demanded Ian.

"Hey! hey!" Francine cut in, "I can tell you what's wrong. That's a value judgment. He was told he *ought* to donate bone marrow."

"Right." Ian's brow furrowed.

"And the reason given for why he ought to do so was a simple fact. The factual statement was that if he didn't donate the bone marrow, his cousin would die."

"Yes!" exclaimed Ted.

"But what's wrong with that reason?" Ian persisted. "It seems like a perfectly good reason for his duty to do it."

"But it's not," replied Ted. "At least not standing alone. You see, the person urging this man to donate bone marrow has jumped directly from a factual statement to a value statement. He seems to think that this factual statement alone supports the value statement and shows it to be true."

"Well, doesn't it?" Ian was insistent.

"No. It only seems like a strong reason to you because you are assuming something else," answered Ted.

Discovering our assumptions

"There he goes, telling me my own assumptions," Ian chortled. "I was warned this might happen if I discussed anything important with a philosopher."

"Hey! Assumptions *are* important," Ted responded. "Whether we know it or not, nearly everything we say assumes something. Most of our assumptions are so basic to our thinking that we have never questioned them. In fact, at times we have to work at it even to discover what they are. In this case you're assuming an in-between step."

"I am?"

"Yes. Didn't you just say that a good reason for this man to donate bone marrow is that if he didn't his cousin would die?"

"Sure."

"You're assuming that it is better for this man's cousin to live than to die."

"Well, of course."

Bridging the gap between facts and values

"No, not of course. That's an assumption, and it's only when you join the factual statement this man was told to this assumption of yours that you have a good reason for thinking the value judgment is true. In other words, if it really is better for this cousin to live than to die, and if not donating the bone marrow would allow him to die, then the man ought to donate it.

"But notice something. That value judgment simply doesn't follow from the factual statement alone. By itself, the fact that not donating bone marrow to him would allow a preventable death tells us nothing about what ought to be done. You need that in-between assumption."

Ian thought hard and then said, "So you're saying that if I had a different assumption, this factual statement might not make the value judgment true at all."

"Precisely," affirmed Ted.

"But how could I? This assumption is so obvious!"

"Look at it this way. Suppose this person concluded that because of some highly unusual circumstances, it would be better for this cousin to die peacefully. Maybe he is in incurable excruciating pain, or maybe he is an Adolf Hitler who has caused the torturous death of millions and would continue to do so if allowed to live. Whatever the reasons might be, for the person who had a different assumption than yours, who assumed it would be better for the cousin to die, the factual statement would no longer be a reason for him to donate bone marrow. In fact, it would be a reason for *not* doing so. It would be a reason for thinking the value judgment was false. If it was better for the cousin to die, and if donating bone marrow would cause him not to die, then he ought *not* to donate bone marrow."

Ian sighed. "So it all depends on the stepping-stone assumption between the factual and value statements."

"Everything hangs on that."

Suddenly Francine chuckled.

"Obviously Francine sees something we don't," Ian remarked. "A special insight, maybe from the world of academia?"

"I was just thinking of something my father told me a few years ago. He wanted me to make something useful of my life and told me I ought to go to college. When I asked him why, he said if I didn't, I'd never get a decent desk job. I'd be stuck waitressing all my life. Well, you can guess which of those appealed to me more at the time. I was young, and all I could think of was all those tips. I certainly had no use for a stuffy office job."

"Perfect example," remarked Ted. "You and your father had different assumptions, and his factual statement combined with your assumption actually gave you a reason for thinking his value judgment was false."

"Right! I remember thinking, *If going to college would get me an office job, and I don't want an office job, then I better not go to college.* The exact opposite of what my father had told me I ought to do."

"And look at her now," Graham quipped. "Francine, the academic success story."

"Hey, it's a free country. I can change an assumption if I decide to."

The inability of facts, alone, to produce moral judgments

"Well, what can we learn from all of this?" Ted inquired. Answering his own question, he continued, "We can learn that a factual statement alone does not provide an adequate reason for thinking a value judgment is true. There is always a bridge premise. To show the value judgment is true, we must not only show that the supporting factual statement is true. That's the easy part. We must also show that the bridge premise between the factual and value statements is true."

"Now you've got me worried," sighed Ian.

"A little scrutiny can go a long way to complicate a nice neat model, can't it, Ian?" joked Graham.

"Okay, hold on!" retorted Ian. "As I recall, your coherence model didn't emerge from scrutiny as a roaring success either. And don't forget, I haven't conceded defeat yet."

At that point Ted leaned forward, rubbing his hands together. "There is a point to all of this," he said. "Let's apply it to Ian's human nature model."

"Oh no. Here goes," said Ian uneasily.

"You did say you welcomed careful scrutiny," said Ted.

"That I did."

"Now then," continued Ted. "The human nature model asserts that we ought not to perform certain acts; for example, we ought not to make slaves of humans. That's a value judgment. When we ask why, we are told it is because those acts violate human nature. That's a factual statement."

"I have to admit, I've never analyzed it that way before," muttered Ian.

"Now's your chance," responded Ted. "And remember, we're all in this thing together looking for truth—no winners, no losers. Now of course, between that factual statement and value judgment is a bridge premise. There always is."

"And I think I've figured out what it is," cut in Francine. "The assumption is that violating human nature is wrong."

"Exactly!" said Ted. "It's the very unstated assumption we pointed out in the first difficulty with Ian's model."

"So it's really the same problem," said Francine.

"Yes, it is," replied Ted. "The important thing to catch here is that not only *do* people who use this model make this assumption, they *must* make it. The model simply doesn't work without it. It bridges the gap between the factual and value claims. In other words, if violating human nature really is wrong, and slavery violates human nature, then of course slavery is wrong and we ought not to practice it. That is the human nature model once we spell it out.

"But watch closely what happens if we meet someone who doesn't hold that same assumption. I mean a person who actually thinks violating human nature is good, or at least not wrong. For this person, the fact that an act violates human nature will be a reason for thinking the act is good— or at least not wrong. It all depends upon the bridge premise."

"I would think then," interjected Francine, "that the primary task of the human nature model would be to support this bridge premise, to prove that violating human nature is wrong."

"You're on the mark there," replied Ted. "That is the fundamental task, and unfortunately it is also the Achilles' heel of the model."

"You mean there is no way to prove this assumption correct?" Ian was incredulous.

Ted chose his words carefully. "Well, think of it this way. It is one thing to know certain actions violate human nature. You've shown us one, slavery."

"Uh-huh."

"And there are others, like dishonesty, which involves using people for one's own purposes, not providing them the information they need to act as fully informed rational agents, while leading them on to think you are."

"I agree."

"My point is," Ted continued, "that the advocate of this model can show us that certain acts violate human nature. That is not difficult.

The difficulty of showing why it is wrong to violate human nature

"However," he said with great emphasis, "the only way to prove these acts are wrong is also to show that it is wrong to violate human nature. But where do we get this information from? There is nothing in human nature itself that tells us it is wrong to violate it. To say it is obvious will not do, because, as we've seen, what is obvious to some is not obvious to others. That is entirely subjective. Even if it appeared obvious to all, that in itself is not a reason, an argument for its being true. Furthermore, we can't look to something else to tell us that violating human nature is wrong, or that other thing then becomes the fundamental explanation for objective moral value."

Ian persisted. "Can't we simply agree together that if something violates human nature, it is wrong?"

"Oh yes, we could," Ted responded. "But then we would no longer have *objective* moral value. We would have only *agreed-upon* value, which is a far cry from what we mean when we speak of something being morally right or wrong objectively. By that we mean that certain acts are wrong and ought to be condemned, and that their wrongness does not depend on the opinion or attitude of any person.

"Isn't that what you meant in that letter you wrote to the newspaper last year condemning the university's policy on harassment?" he asked Francine. "You weren't overly concerned with whether or not others agreed with you, right?"

She nodded.

"The policy's wrongness did not depend upon any consensus among individuals."

"You're right. That is what I meant."

Ted looked up at the group. "It looks, then, as if we are going to have to look for a different way of explaining objective moral value. The human nature model doesn't provide us with an adequate explanation. We are left without a reason for thinking human nature should be the ground of objective moral value. It does not tell us why violating human nature is inevitably and invariably wrong. Why should this be the standard or criterion for all moral right and wrong? Nor, for that matter, has it told us why it is that all wrong acts are wrong because somehow, in some way, they involve a violation of human nature."

"So human nature does not provide an adequate foundation for truly objective moral value," Ian stated dejectedly.

"I'm afraid you're right," said Ted.

"Well, then, where shall we look for this elusive foundation?" asked Graham.

"There is another option we secular humanists put forward," answered Ian.

"But I thought you just gave us your view," exclaimed Graham.

"I did, but there is more than one way a secular humanist could account for objective moral value. I've given you one."

"And we've seen how it's held up under scrutiny."

"If Ian has another explanation, I for one would like to hear him out," invited Ted, "but our time is up. You've got a whole week to work on your viewpoint, Ian."

After quick farewells, they were off in different directions, each being driven by a separate car and driver.

The discussion had been stimulating, the surroundings impressive, but a nagging question was beginning to emerge in some of their minds. A foundation for objective moral standards must exist. It had to. The world would hardly make sense without it. But, one by one, their attempts to find one were being found wanting.

Ted, however, had another intriguing question on his mind. As the car swept through the gate, he had an idea and quickly memorized the house number on the gatepost.

9
CAN OUR NEEDS
BE THE BASIS
OF MORALS?
A Humanist Foundation, Part II

nother week went quickly as Ted lectured, met with
students and graded papers. Constantly on his mind
was the address on the gatepost at the big house. He
decided to have a title search done on the property.

It proved to be registered in the name of a male at the
same address. The only thing that stood out to him about
the name was that it meant nothing to him. *Who is this
mystery person?* he wondered, *and how did he know about me?*

He thought about mentioning the name to the doorkeeper, but in the end his desire not to be seen as nosy prevailed. He did want to find out who was responsible for
these discussions, but not if it would cause an uncomfort-

able incident. Besides, today Ian would try for the second time to provide a secular humanist foundation for objective moral standards. *After last week's dismantling of his view, I'm sure he'll be prepared,* Ted chuckled to himself.

The doorkeeper led Ted to the reception room efficiently, with a minimum of conversation. Ian and the others were at the far end of the room. Francine was closest to the serving table and asked, "So what will it be? Coffee for everyone?"

"I say let's start the day out right," smiled Ted as he quickly held a cup up to her. The others turned to greet him, and they all welcomed the hot coffee.

"It takes the chill out of that cool, windy weather," remarked William.

"I would have thought a Brit like you would have preferred tea," commented Ian.

"Oh no!" shot back William. "When in Rome . . ."

"Yes, yes."

Everyone seemed to be in good spirits. Even Ian had bounced back after the bruising that followed his first attempt to give a foundation for objective moral value. After some small talk, the discussion turned to the issue at hand.

"Are we ready to continue our search?" Graham asked. "We're looking for something that so far has proven to be highly elusive, and yet its importance can hardly be overstated."

"You mean an explanation for objective moral value," interjected Francine.

"That's it. We've seen that none of us can deny it exists. In fact, once we realize the implications of life without it, few if any of us will want to escape it. And don't forget that things must have adequate explanations for their existence. Ted made sure we saw that earlier."

The necessity of causes

"Your point, of course," added Francine, "is that somewhere there must be an adequate explanation for objective moral value."

"Absolutely," Ted joined in. "But what it is we have not

yet discovered."

"We do know, however, that the human nature explanation does not succeed in explaining it," quipped Graham.

"You would have to remind us!" Ian fired back. "Just don't forget what else we learned a couple of weeks back. Your coherence model didn't emerge from the scrutiny very impressively either."

"I'd like to forget."

"Which leads us directly back to you," said Ted, looking at Ian with his customary twinkle. "If I recall, last week you were about to tell us of another way of explaining objective moral value. You've had a week to ruminate on it."

"Yes," Graham added, sarcasm dripping from each word. "Please grace us with your pearls of wisdom."

"Still miffed, are you?" Ian retorted.

"Hey! I'm all ears."

With that Ian sat up straight and began, enforcing each point by cutting the air with a sharp jab. "If we called my first theory the human nature explanation, we could call this one the human need explanation."

"Catchy!" said Graham.

"But then again," Ian continued, "we may want to call it the social contract model."

"Decisive, too!" Graham again interjected.

Unfazed, Ian continued, "When I explain, you'll see why both could work." Ian knew he was about to set out one of the most common attempts to account for objective moral value. The problem was that it involved the ideas of both human needs and of social agreement. Hence it was difficult to choose one of them for a title.

Graham was impatient. "So how does this explanation work?"

Ian continued. "This model states that objective moral value is rooted not in human nature but in human needs. Think about it. Human beings have certain basic needs that must be met if we are going to survive, much less flourish."

"Such as?" pressed Graham.

*Could human
needs be the basis
of morality?*

"We need honesty. We need trust, fair treatment, respect for human life and so forth. Can you imagine a group of human beings trying to live together where these were not present? Imagine a situation where no one thought anything strange or wrong about torturing and killing others at will, where one would deceive another as a normal way of life."

"It would be nasty," Graham concurred.

"It would be much worse than that! They could never communicate with each other. They could never count on anyone for anything. Life itself would be short at the best of times, because no one would think it strange to assure you that they would not harm you and then do just that the moment your back was turned."

Social contract "My point is this. If human beings are going to survive, certain standards of behavior must be established among them. My social contract explanation says that based on these needs which humans find themselves having, humans come together and agree to call certain sorts of behavior good and others bad. They attach the labels of moral or immoral to those kinds of conduct which are seen to be highly important to the social well-being of the group."

"Very interesting!" replied Francine enthusiastically. "This would explain why moral codes have had some basic similarities every place and every time we find human beings. I'm thinking of the UN Declaration of Human Rights which Ted spoke of."

"And the ancient moral codes," added Graham, somewhat less cynical than a moment ago.

"Exactly!" responded Ian. "Since human needs are basically the same wherever and whenever we find them, we would expect that the moral laws stemming from those needs would also have much in common. And we've seen that they do."

"And you are saying," Ted asked, "that social agreement based on these needs can explain objective moral value?"

"That is what I'm saying," replied Ian rather boldly. He knew what lay ahead—criticism and scrutiny—so he was temporarily relieved to hear Ted's next suggestion.

"I say we should break for lunch before examining Ian's view. Maybe the blood will flow more freely."

"Not to mention the adrenaline," Francine quipped. Ian was optimistic, however, about his new foundation.[1]

After lunch, Ted spoke up. "Here we have it: a new way of explaining objective moral value. And of course we must ask if it succeeds any better than the others we've looked into." Then, looking at Ian he asked, "You *will* entertain questions, won't you?"

"Fair is fair," he responded cheerfully.

Francine leaned forward, choosing her words carefully. "This approach has a certain appeal to me. It seems to make sense. I mean, we humans do have certain needs, and our moral standards do serve those needs."

"So far I like your reaction!" said Ian enthusiastically. "But I thought you were a moral relativist. Don't you believe there is no such thing as objective moral value? That we're all barking up the wrong tree here in trying to explain it?"

"Oh, don't get me wrong. I do have more questions!" she shot back firmly.

"Somehow I thought so."

"For instance," Francine continued, "let's just suppose all of you are right, that it does exist after all. Are you sure your approach will really explain *objective* moral value?" She placed great emphasis on the word *objective*.

"Why wouldn't it?" Ian queried.

Turning to Ted, Francine continued, "How exactly did we define objective moral value earlier?"

"An important question," he answered. "You'll recall that both of the two views we've examined so far foundered on this point. The moral value they were able to explain was not really *objective* moral value." He too placed great stress on the word.

"Let me get this straight," Graham cut in. "We are supposing that a group of people—be it two, three, ten or any number—come together and agree that an act is right or wrong."

"Yes."

"And we are asking whether their agreement alone makes that act right or wrong in an objective sense."

"Precisely."

Objective
morality defined

"And that's where I see a problem emerging," interjected Francine, picking up where she had left off. "Earlier we saw that objective value means that the rightness or wrongness of an action is not dependent on the opinion or belief of any person. If it were, then we would have only *subjective* moral value. In other words, the morality of an action would depend solely on the belief or opinion of the subjects, the persons involved."

"She's right!" responded Ted. "Always remember that if an action is objectively wrong, it will not matter who agrees or disagrees with that judgment. That is what *objective* means. And that is precisely why we feel justified in condemning certain acts as wrong, like race discrimination, rape, dishonesty, tax evasion and others, regardless of what others think. If these were only subjectively wrong, it would merely be the opinion of some person or persons that they were wrong. Others would be equally entitled to their opinions, and their opinions would be equally justified and correct."[2]

Is social contract
morality
objective
morality?

Sensing that his explanation was under attack, Ian spoke up. "So you are saying my explanation will not account for objective moral value, only subjective?"

"I'm afraid it looks that way," replied Ted.

A grim expression settled on Ian's face.

"Think of it this way," Ted continued. "You are admitting up front, are you not, that any wrong action is wrong for no other reason than that people have agreed to call it wrong?"

"Right," Ian responded. "But the reason they call it wrong is that they have seen that it will serve our human needs better to do so."

"Yes, but that doesn't change the fact that it still rests on a decision by people about what is right and wrong."

"I know that," persisted Ian, "but again I repeat we are agreeing about that because we've seen that we serve human needs better this way."

"I understand," said Ted. "But that is different from their being right and wrong in a truly objective sense. On your explanation, a society decides that what serves their needs is important enough to be considered morally right or wrong. It all rests on their decision about what they regard as important."[3]

Ian nodded but said nothing.

Ted continued. "What you are *not*—I repeat *not*—saying is that actions such as lying, raping and harming others are wrong in themselves and that we are simply recognizing their wrongness. You see, that's what objective right and wrong would mean. If an act is wrong in an objective sense, it is wrong not because we agree together to designate it as wrong, whatever our reason for doing so may be. Quite the contrary. We simply recognize it as being wrong apart from anyone's designation. Only then do we feel justified in condemning others for performing such acts."

"In other words," Ian continued, "you're telling me that this explanation has the same problem as my human nature model had. It only accounts for what we were calling 'agreed-upon value.' "

"I'm afraid you're right," replied Ted. "Agreed-upon value is a far cry from the objective value we are trying to account for."

After a few moments to digest this new turn of events, Graham asked, "On this explanation, couldn't a group of people conceivably agree together to designate almost any action right or wrong if they found those actions to suit them better?"

"That sounds dangerous," mused Francine.

"Actually, it's more than dangerous," affirmed Ted. "As a matter of fact, whenever we're dealing with agreed-upon values, that is a live possibility. Those agreeing together can literally agree on any moral code, and if the agreement alone is what makes the code correct, then any agreed-upon code will be right by definition."

Can social contract morality condemn anything?

Ted continued. "As bizarre as it sounds, for purposes of our discussion here, let's imagine a group of people who decide together that it would be better for the rest of us if all university professors were jailed indefinitely."

"That thought has occurred to me," said Francine with a smirk.

The sole requirement: agreement

"And to others, I'm sure," Ted replied knowingly. "But if this were to happen, what could the professors say? To complain that this sort of treatment is just not right would be futile. If Ian's explanation is true, if *agreement* alone is what makes it right, then of course it's right. The group has agreed to it. It doesn't matter *what* they agree to, because no act is right or wrong in itself. Morality is decided strictly by the agreement by the group."

At that moment Francine raised her eyebrows and in cool investigative style queried, "Could I ask who decides on the morality of actions?"

Ian looked perplexed. "Maybe I'm missing something here," he said, "but I don't get the question."

Francine continued. "You're speaking of this social agreement on the rightness or wrongness of certain actions."

"Right."

"You're saying that people have agreed on this."

"Uh-huh."

"Well, I'm asking which people."

Whose agreement is required?

Ian nodded. He hadn't expected this line of questioning. At one time he might have said all of us agree, but now he could see that answer would never satisfy this crowd. Disagreement exists between people. Perfect consensus will never be achieved. But whose agreement is required?

"Francine's question is an important one," Ted remarked. "In the lecture we saw that many similarities exist in moral ideas among humankind. However, we also know that there is some disagreement, whether it be small groups disagreeing with the masses or an entire country adopting a different moral stance from others'."

"You mean like Hitler's Germany?" piped up Francine.

They all nodded.

Ted continued. "Our question now is, if agreement among people makes an act right or wrong, whose agreement is required? Is it the agreement of the greatest number of people? the wisest? the strongest? the most powerful? And how do we decide? Do you provide criteria along with your explanation?" He directed this last question to Ian.

Ian shook his head, muttering to himself.

After pausing to let his questions sink in, Ted continued. "But that's only one problem with it. There's another."

Ian seemed to cringe.

"What will we do," asked Ted, "when two groups of people agree to different, conflicting moral codes? In other words, they differ as to what they will call right and wrong. Who will judge between them? For instance, what if the professors I just mentioned decided that it would serve the needs of most other people better for them not only to stay out of jail but also to receive room and board paid for out of the public coffers? This could be in return for certain services, such as regular public lectures to help in the intellectual development of society."

Graham rolled his eyes. "Now that idea has never occurred to me, I must confess," he retorted.

"But this is a group of people, and they did agree together on this."

Then Ted leaned forward and spoke intently. "You see," he said, "if agreement alone is necessary, then presumably both of these moral codes will be right. But of course they cannot both be right, because they contradict one other."

Conflicting moral codes cannot both be right

Ian nodded. He could see that there really were no clear answers to these questions.

Suddenly, however, he spoke up, looking distraught but not defeated. "All right, you've leveled some stiff charges against my social contract model. You've said it accounts for agreed-upon but not objective value. You're also telling me it could allow for virtually any moral code and that it provides no way of judging between conflicting moral codes."

"He's a good listener," Graham quipped.

"But," Ian continued, raising his hand, "it's time for rebuttal. My model won't allow for agreement on just any moral code. I am arguing that the actions agreed to be wrong are specifically those that violate human needs. The right ones are those that serve our needs. So I do have a standard to judge by after all."

"A worthwhile point," nodded Ted.

"I'm glad you like it."

"But before you get too excited, I have a question for you about your standard."

"I'm sure you do."

"My question is, where did you get it from?"

"Come again?" Ian looked bewildered.

The arbitrariness of human need

"Let me put it this way," Ted continued. "Why *this* standard? Exactly why is it that violating human needs is what makes an act wrong?"

Ian began to think fast, knowing he would need a response in very short order.

"True, human need is your standard," Ted went on, "but what is the basis for it? Why couldn't a group of people reject your standard and choose another, or even no standard at all? What reason is there for them to choose yours?"

Ian had anticipated this question but now was wondering just how adequate his answer would be for this crowd. Cautiously he replied, "That is simply part of what is agreed to."

The human need standard: agreement

Ted raised his eyebrows inquisitively but said nothing, so Ian continued. "Those who agree together to designate certain acts as right or wrong also agree on the standard to guide them. They agree together that actions that violate human need ought to be designated as wrong and the others not. What's wrong with that?"

"Just one thing," replied Ted. "It's creative, but I'm afraid it won't help."

"Why not?"

"Think carefully about it. If your standard is merely agreed to, then it has the same weaknesses we've already seen. You see, you still have only 'agreed-upon' value."

"But I have a standard!" Ian shot back.

"Yes, but now the standard on which your moral rules are based is only part of what is agreed to. Those who agreed to it could have chosen a different one and been equally correct."

Ian nodded but said nothing.

"This means that even with your standard, there is still no reason that any group of people could not agree on any moral code whatsoever, as we said earlier. If the standard itself is part of what they agree to, they could simply choose a different one from what you have chosen. That would then allow them to designate as wrong any act that violates their standard. Remember, if agreement on the standard is all that is required, then any agreed-upon standard would be equally justified."

Graham spoke up, his eyes flashing. "And don't we still have the problem of who decides on the standard and what to do when two groups of people decide on different standards?"

"I'm afraid so," affirmed Ted. "Those same problems apply to the standard too, if it is only part of what is agreed to."

Ian was more than a little taken back. "So my model still does not account for objective moral value but only for 'agreed-upon' value?"

Ted nodded his agreement. "So far it looks that way."

After a few sips of his coffee, Graham glanced over at Ian. He was just about to give him a verbal jab when he noticed a smile on his face. "Ian must know something the rest of us don't," he commented.

"Maybe I do," he said.

"Please enlighten us." Graham's hands were extended in a welcoming fashion.

"I was just thinking," Ian said. "There may be a way to save my explanation after all."

Graham was taken aback. "You mean you think there is

still a way it can account for objective value, after all we've heard?"

"Maybe so," Ian replied. "It all has to do with my standard, human need. Remember when Ted asked me what basis there was for my standard?"

"Yes, and you said it was simply agreed to as part of the social contract."

"Yes, I did, but maybe there's another answer to that question."

"Which is?"

Is violating human needs objectively wrong?

"Couldn't I answer that the basis for the human need standard is that violating human needs is really, objectively wrong regardless of what anyone thinks? In that case my model would simply recognize this fact and argue that acts that violate human needs are objectively wrong for that reason. That would also mean that a group of people could not simply agree to any other standard, as you were saying they could. If they did so, they would be wrong. This is the one correct standard. If you violate human needs your action is wrong, objectively wrong."

"That is a highly interesting move," said Ted. "Let me see if I follow it. You are now admitting that social agreement alone will not establish that something is objectively right or wrong?"

"Yes, I am. I suppose I have to admit that it can only account for 'agreed-upon' value, not objective value. But that's precisely my point now. I am not arguing for a social agreement alone. I am arguing that in this social agreement, people agree that certain acts violate human needs and that's what makes them wrong."

"So," said Ted, "it's now the violation of human need that really is objctively wrong?"

"Right."

"And those who agree on which acts are right and wrong simply recognize this fact and then agree about which acts do this."

"Exactly."

"Ingenious!" remarked Ted.

Ian brightened. "I'm glad you're impressed."

"And it does solve the problems raised earlier with the social contract model," agreed Ted.

"Please keep talking!"

"However," Ted raised his hand, "unfortunately it also raises another set of problems."

"There's always a fly in the ointment," groaned Ian. "New problems."

"Well, not actually new ones. One of them is the same problem we raised for Graham's coherence explanation. Remember our discussion on that?"

"How could we forget?" muttered Graham.

"Then you'll recall that one of the problems with that explanation," continued Ted, "was that it did not really explain why moral principles were objectively true. It simply began with them. Remember the moral truisms, as Graham called them? Starting with them as brute facts is far different from explaining why they are there in the first place."[4]

"And you're saying I am making the same mistake?" asked Ian.

"I'm afraid so."

"How?"

"Didn't you just say that you are now beginning with the assertion that violating human nature is objectively wrong?"

"Uh-huh."

"Well, that is different from telling us *why* it is objectively wrong. You are actually setting this up as a moral truism, to borrow Graham's terminology. Then you derive the rest of your moral code from there. But you have not explained any foundation for this one truism."

*Another
unfounded moral
truism*

Ian sat quietly, his brow furrowed.

Suddenly Francine spoke up. "Doesn't Ian's new procedure also run into the same problem we saw with his human nature explanation?"

"Which one?" inquired Ian.

"The question of what made the violation of human nature objectively wrong. Remember our discussion about the distinction between facts and values? What were we calling it, the fact-value problem?"[5]

"Good memory!" affirmed Ted.

"And are you now saying that my human need model will run into the same fact-value problem?" Ian asked.

"I don't see how it can avoid it," answered Francine. "As I recall, it was one thing to show an action violated human nature and quite another to show that violating human nature is wrong."

"That's right," Ted added. "We saw that there is nothing in human nature which tells us that violating it is wrong. And as we said, it seems like the ultimate in arbitrary preferential treatment to select our species on which all morality hinges without some basis.

Deriving moral truth from facts about human needs   "But now notice that the same problems exist here with your human need model. It is one thing to show that an act violates human need; that's a factual statement. But it's quite another to show that violating human needs is wrong; that is a value statement. The problem is that unless we can show that violating human needs is wrong, neither can we show that acts that do it are wrong."

"And," added Graham, "I imagine that showing the wrongness of violating human needs will be no easier than it was for human nature."

"Yes, it will be just as hard, and for the same reasons," agreed Ted. "You see, again there is nothing in human needs themselves that tells us it is wrong to violate them. To say it is obvious will never do, because what is obvious to one is not to others. And even if it were obvious to all, that still would not provide an explanation for its wrongness, only agreement on it. And if some other thing tells us this is wrong, then that other thing is the real ground of objective moral value. In the end we will be left with the same question about giving ourselves arbitrary preferential treatment. Why *human* needs? I can hear the animal rights supporter now: 'How convenient!' "

"It looks to me," said Graham, "like we're going back to simply agreeing together that violating human needs is wrong. Which, of course, can only account for what we're calling 'agreed-upon' value, not truly objective value."

"It seems so," said Ted, leaning back.

"And so," said Ian, "regrettably, our search for an adequate explanation for objective moral value continues.

"I can't help but wonder," he continued, "if we can be sure that there is an adequate explanation for it. What if there just isn't one? Let's face it. We've been through three attempts now."

Ted chuckled. "Ian, I'm surprised. After all this time."

"Hey! If there isn't one, then we're involved in a futile exercise, looking for something that doesn't exist. All these lunches, chauffeured rides, discussions. What for?" Ian raised his hands in frustration.

"That would be futile all right, but I don't think you have to worry. Notice what that would mean. It would mean that something exists, objective value, without a cause of its existence."

"But we've already covered that!" Graham shot back. "We saw pretty clearly awhile ago that nothing happens or exists without an adequate cause for its existence."

"And in fact," Ted added, "there's a widely accepted principle that states this. It's called the principle of sufficient reason. It states that nothing cannot produce something."

Graham chuckled at the very thought. "I should say not!"

Ted went on. "There must be a cause for all things' coming into existence, including objective moral value."

Ian sighed. "I guess I'm just getting a little discouraged."

"But don't be!" Ted exclaimed. "We now know three commonly tried explanations that are wrong. That's progress!"

"Now that's a new twist on it." Graham smiled.

"I think we've got an eternal optimist here," said Ian.

"But my optimism isn't merely a character trait that endures in spite of the facts. I'm optimistic because we've made real progress here. Which means we have every reason to believe we'll make more."

"But will we achieve our goal?" Ian persisted. "Will we discover an adequate explanation for objective moral value?"

Ted looked directly at Ian and replied, "There is no reason to think we won't."

At that moment William's face lit up. "There is another explanation that hasn't been mentioned yet."

"Oh, some new insights from the field of evolution?" crowed Ian.

"As a matter of fact, yes. Since none of your explanations have been adequate, I'd like to put one on the table. I learned it in my university days. I'm beginning to think it may be the strongest yet. Of course I'll have to dig through some dusty old notes to brush up on it."

"Aren't we contemporary now!" Ian said sarcastically.

"We've already agreed that we don't tell truth by the clock, or the calendar," reminded William. "I believe Ted made that point when we first met. Right, Ted?"

"Absolutely!" exclaimed Ted, emphasizing each syllable.

"The fact that my explanation may be older than yours," William continued, "is irrelevant to the question of whether it's true. For that you have to hear my view and examine it."

"Okay! Okay!" Ian held up both hands with palms out. "Correction taken."

Ted glanced at his watch. "Our time is up, but it looks like we've got our topic for next time."

As Ted left the house and stepped into the waiting car, his thoughts began to drift. It was interesting how they had all come to view the meetings as normal and how the rest of the group had almost ceased questioning who was behind these discussions and what this person might want. *How much we accept,* he mused, *without really thinking it through, without good reasons.*

10
MORALS—THE KEY TO SURVIVAL
An Evolutionary Foundation

T ed wasn't sure where to search next to find out who the mystery host was. He wasn't used to being a detective. He mentioned the name from the title search to a couple of colleagues, but they didn't recognize it either. Nor was it listed in the phone book.

But there was something else. He wasn't even sure anymore that he wanted to pursue the matter. On the one hand he was dying to find out who had orchestrated what had turned into a successful series of luncheons. On the other hand he had become comfortable with the arrangement and didn't want to disrupt it. The week's events had conspired against him. He had just been too busy, so he promised himself he'd get to the bottom of it very soon.

Meanwhile William was on his way to the mansion. His thoughts returned to the discussions of the past few weeks.

He had to admit he really believed evolution provided a foundation for objective moral value—a foundation that was superior to anything presented so far. It seemed to answer most of the difficulties that had brought the others down. However, he also knew he was in for some serious scrutiny. He had been quiet during much of the discussion so far. Now he would try his own version. But this crowd could be ruthless, especially as an ever-increasing number of them had been humiliated by having their own explanations disproved. Nonetheless, as the car turned into the driveway, he felt prepared and confident.

When he arrived, he found his partners in discussion in the same familiar room. The chairs were in a circle. An inviting fire crackled in the fireplace, creating an atmosphere of warmth. *Perfect for discussion,* he thought to himself. *Everyone should be in a generous mood.*

After the usual small talk, the room quieted, and Ted spoke up. "If my memory serves me well, I believe William has a new explanation for objective moral value to share with us."

"Indeed I do."

"The man exudes confidence," remarked Ian. "This should be good."

"We've examined the coherence model, the human nature model and the human need model," said Ted. "What are you calling your explanation?"

"All right," said William, rubbing his hands with nervous energy. "Mine is the evolutionary model."

"That's creative," Ian muttered. "Sounds like you're taking us off in a brand-new direction. I'm afraid I'm no expert on evolution and certainly haven't formed an opinion on its merits yet."

"And you won't need to," replied the evolutionist. "You do know that it teaches that every species of plant and animal, including us, developed into its present form from an original, very primitive state. This change from a primitive being to a more specialized one happened through slight changes being transmitted successively from one generation to the next."

Ian nodded. "And doesn't it also teach that many species went extinct over these millions of years while all this evolution was taking place?"

"Right. Who said you weren't an expert?" William laughed. "Throughout this process, any kind of plant or animal that couldn't survive didn't. Every species either adapted and changed to become survivable or it went extinct. Sometimes this is called the survival of the fittest."

"I see," Ian mused. "And that's where the change comes in. As they adapted and changed to survive, new forms of life were continually coming into being."

"Right again. And every species alive today has what it needs to survive as a result of this evolutionary process."[1]

"But," asked Ted, "how does any of this help us explain the existence of objective moral value? I take it you're going to tell us that this evolutionary process can account for it in some way?"

Morality, necessary for survival

"Precisely."

"But before you do," Francine interrupted, "back to Ian's question. What if I don't accept evolution in the first place? Which I don't! In my opinion there are just too many problems with it. If all forms of life arose from one ancestor, then what did *it* arise from? We've already seen that things don't come from nothing. And the fossil record. Correct me if I'm wrong, but as I see it, that is a *real* problem. If an evolutionary process occurred, there should be millions of transitional forms between the various forms of life they ancestrally link together, but they have never been found."

"Hold on!" cried William. "I never said you have to accept it. In fact, you don't, at least not for now."

Francine shook her head. "I'm a little perplexed. If we work through your model, whatever it is, aren't we supposing that things really did come into existence this way?"

"Yes, we are."

"That's where you lose me," she huffed.

"It's simple, really. In each of the explanations so far we have been supposing certain things, but only for the purpose of discussion. For instance, Ian had us supposing that morality began with humans agreeing together about it. We assumed, for purposes of discussion, that morality began that way and then went on to test that theory to see if that sort of foundation for morality could account for the morality we see around us today. And we saw it could not, so we discarded the assumption."

"Don't remind me," Ian groaned.

"And," continued Francine, "you are telling us to suppose that the world began the way evolution says it did, but for now it's only an assumption for purposes of our discussion."

"Exactly. My model asks, If things did come into existence through this long process of evolution, could that process account for objective moral value? In other words, could objective value be the result of an evolutionary process?"

"But it still seems to me," countered Francine, "that if it can account for objective value better than any alternative, then that in itself will be a strong argument for evolution."

"Good observation. Of course it's a bigger question than that, and there are other reasons to be considered."

Ted cleared his throat and turned to William. "Let's try again. Exactly how would this evolutionary process account for objective moral value?"

"Here's how," he replied. "We've agreed that humans everywhere have certain moral ideas. Things are judged to be morally right or wrong by people everywhere."

They all nodded quietly.

"In other words, there is universal moral knowledge or awareness."

"Right," Ted replied. "That's what we've been trying to account for all along."

Morality, a biological adaptation

"My model," William continued, "argues that this moral awareness is a biological adaptation, a product of the evolutionary process we just spoke of. All humans have moral awareness because this awareness is of biological worth. We need it to survive."

"Ingenious!" interrupted Graham. "Why didn't I think of that? And I believe in evolution too. We atheists tend to prefer it as a way to account for the origin of the world."

"Well, then, I'm sure you'll like my foundation. It states that the moral awareness we all have is just like our hands, feet and teeth. You see," William continued, pointing to his teeth with one hand and waving the other, "according to the theory of evolution, these developed over the long evolutionary process as an adaptation making it possible for us to survive. Without them we couldn't stay alive. We would have been one of the species that went extinct."

"Hmm," Graham murmured. "That much I'm familiar with. But you're introducing a new idea about evolution, aren't you?"

"Yes, I am. But it makes just as much sense as the ideas you're already familiar with. What I'm adding is that we couldn't survive without moral awareness any better than we could without hands, feet or teeth. Think about it. Can you imagine a group of people living together who had no sense whatsoever that it was morally wrong to kill other humans for no reason? Or to be dishonest as a normal way of living? Or to act unfairly most of the time?"

"Didn't we already cover this?" asked Graham.

"We certainly did. The same question came up in Ian's human need model. Remember, he was trying to show that humans need moral guidelines to survive and flourish, so they come together and agree on some."

"So much for that theory," Graham chuckled.

"Okay, okay!" said Ian. "But isn't there something to my point about humans needing morality in order to live and function together?"

"I think there is," said William, "and that's my whole point here. We do need it. It's an aid to human survival and reproduction. We couldn't get along without it. What's more, it's pretty clear that we all have moral awareness. Now if we didn't get it by simply agreeing on it, as we saw last week, then we must have come upon it some other way. My model says this moral awareness developed as a biological adaptation no less than our other adaptations. Any beings like us who didn't develop this moral sense would have gone extinct because they lacked something necessary for survival.[2]

"Let me explain further about how this works in actual practice," he went on. "The most fundamental moral disposition in humans is the affection of a parent for his or her child. Without this the child could never survive. And this affection elicits a responding desire in the child to please its parents. Out of this relationship the child begins to develop a sense of empathy, fairness and self-control and acquires a conscience that makes him or her behave out of a sense of duty. As time goes on, a broadening occurs, and these moral tendencies are extended to others."[3]

"An intriguing model," Ted commented.

William leaned back in his chair confidently. He was becoming more sure than ever that his was the strongest explanation yet. *Of course,* he thought to himself, *you do ultimately have to accept evolution as a whole if you are to accept my model. But don't most people believe it anyway?*

His thoughts were interrupted by Ted's next remark. "Well stated, William! Not only clear but logical too. But will it succeed as a moral foundation? Let's put it to the test."

Francine sat up in her chair. Looking directly at William, she said, "As ingenious as this model is, I have to ask, does your model account for moral value that is truly *objective?*"

William looked at Francine very intently, brow furrowed. "My answer may surprise you," he said. "No, it does not."

A collective gasp went up.

"But doesn't that discount it altogether? I mean, we are searching for a way to account for objective moral value here. If your explanation doesn't do it, it must be inadequate."

"Not really!" William replied, raising his hand firmly.

"That's where my model is more interesting than the others.

"If my model could speak, it would say something like this: 'I am not here to account for the existence of objective moral value, as you hoped I would. In fact, I don't really think there is any such thing existing out there independent of human beings.' "

Moral adaptation, not objective morality

Graham was incredulous. "But I thought . . ."

"Just hear me out."

"But we agreed a long time ago," Graham continued, barely able to contain his frustration, "that we were looking for a foundation for objective moral value. Now you're telling us, after all this time, that you don't even think there is such a thing. What kind of foundation for objective value is this if you don't even think it exists?"

"As I said, my model doesn't attempt to explain objective moral value. Rather, it explains the feeling, the sense that we humans have that there is objective moral value out there. You see, my model distinguishes between *objective moral value* itself on the one hand and *our sense* that there is objective moral value on the other."

"And you are asserting up front that objective moral value does not exist?"

"I am."

"And your model supposedly explains why all humans have this moral sense, this idea that objective moral value exists out there?"

"Exactly. You see, in my opinion it's not really objective moral value that needs to be explained. Rather, it is the sense, the idea we humans have that there is objective moral value, that needs to be accounted for. The question we should be asking is not why there is objective moral value, but why there is this universal moral sense in humans. My evolutionary model attempts to account for that moral sense in our human psyches."

"I must admit," said Graham, "this is an entirely new approach to our question."

"But if it works, I think we'll have accounted for all we

need to." William smiled.

At that moment Francine intervened. "Discussion is good for the mind, but we have physical needs as well. One without the other is unbalanced."

With that they all moved toward the table, which, as usual, was beautifully laden with pastries, cheeses and a variety of beverages.

After a while Francine looked over at William. "Something else troubles me about your foundation."

"Fire away!"

"If I hear you right, you are telling us that this moral sense was developed so we could survive and reproduce as a species. In fact, aren't you saying that the need to survive is the very impetus for our moral convictions?"

"Yes, I am."

"In other words," Francine continued, "over time humans began to attach moral significance to acts and practices that would promote the survival of the human species?"

"Precisely."

"We began to regard actions that would destroy or hinder our survival as immoral and those that would promote it as morally good?"

William had to laugh. "You're saying it better than I could. So what's the problem?"

Evolutionary morality: unable to account for the sense of duty to care for the weak

"The problem is that if our moral convictions really do stem from the need to do whatever promotes the species, then shouldn't we have the moral conviction that it is right, even our duty, to exterminate the sick, the aged, the handicapped?"

William was momentarily surprised by the question. "That sounds harsh!" he exclaimed. "Why should my model lead to that?"

"Well, you would have to agree, these people don't promote the survival of the human race. In fact, they're a drain on it. They use up resources we all need to survive. They themselves contribute nothing to the survival of our race. And wouldn't it be our duty to get rid of anyone who might contaminate the gene pool—say, people with hereditary chromosomal defects? Shouldn't we at least prohibit them from reproducing? But we as humans have not and do not regard these harsh measures as our duty. In fact we have the opposite convictions. We would condemn anyone who did them."

"I don't agree," William shot back.

"Well, then, tell me where I'm wrong!" Francine pressed.

"I don't believe that a morality stemming from the need to survive as a species would necessarily lead us to regard these harsh actions as our duty. In fact, we don't regard them as such, yet we have managed to survive. We are able to be compassionate to the weak, the aged and the handicapped. We are able to allow all people to reproduce even though some will contaminate the gene pool. We can do all of that and still survive."

Francine thought for a minute, then said, "True, but what I'm asking is whether your evolutionary model could account for the moral convictions we all in fact do have toward these groups. After all, that is what your model is claiming to do—account for the moral convictions we find among human beings."

"Right."

"So then," continued Francine, "the question is, does your model account for the strong moral sense we humans have that it is wrong in the extreme to harm the weak, the aged and the handicapped?"

William listened but said nothing.

"What you're saying, Francine," Ted interjected, "is that there is nothing in a survival-based morality which would produce this strong moral conviction we have against the very actions that would promote the survival of the species."

"That is my point, exactly."

A heavy silence settled over the room. Ted added more wood to the fire, which had burned down to a bed of red-hot embers. Suddenly, glancing over at William, Francine noticed a hint of a smile flickering on his face.

"I didn't expect to see you smiling!" she exclaimed. "What can be funny now?"

His smile widened. "Maybe it could," he murmured.

"Maybe it could what?" she persisted.

"Well"—he paused—"Ted just said that there is nothing in my survival-based morality which would produce the strong convictions most of us have against harming those who are a drain on our species."

"Yes, we all heard him say that."

Could evolutionary development produce our moral convictions?

"But maybe there is a way it *could* account for this conviction," he declared. With each word, his confidence increased.

"How could it?"

Care for the weak: necessary for survival?

"Well, think of it this way. Isn't compassion for those needy, weaker members also necessary for the survival of our species? Who knows, that could be me some day in that weak, sickly condition. Or you."

"How exciting," Ian grumbled.

"But it's true!" William emphasized. "And maybe part of surviving is taking care of our weaker members. In that case the evolutionary process would attach moral duty to doing just that."

"Very resourceful," Ted cut in, "but I'm afraid it will run into the same difficulty we just saw."

"How?"

Ted chuckled. "Let me explain. You are claiming that compassionate treatment for those who are a drain on our species is necessary for our survival, but is it? I don't think so, and here's why. This kindness does make life more pleasant for the weaker members, and it is nice for us all to know that we would receive that kindness too if we were there."

"I agree," said William.

"However," Ted continued, "it is definitely not necessary for human survival. We could survive as a species just fine without it. In fact, if it's only survival we're thinking of, we would be better off without that kind of compassion. Our chances of long-term survival would be increased. All those resources, funds and energy would be freed up for use by the rest of us healthier ones.

"But as Francine pointed out, that is not our attitude. We actually regard it as good to expend resources on needy people, even when it could work against the survival of our species. We use up resources and spend great amounts of money and time which the rest of us could use. And what's more, we do this even when the people concerned will never contribute anything to our survival. I mean people such as the comatose, the mentally handicapped and others. And if we ever do decide it is better to let a person die rather than extend his life with extraordinary means, we do so only with great reluctance and soul-searching. There seems to be nothing in an evolutionary explanation which can explain these strong moral sentiments."

William folded his hands and thought quietly. He had to admit it was difficult to see how his evolutionary model would ever produce these moral convictions. He also knew that any adequate explanation of objective moral value would have to do just that.

Suddenly Graham got up from his chair and began pacing the floor. "Something else troubles me about your evolutionary model," he remarked, nodding in William's direction.

William looked up. "Why should you have a problem with it? This fits perfectly with your atheism."

"Oh, we've already seen my moral foundation, and this isn't it. I'll tell you why. My question is whether anyone really believes your model."

"I do!" William declared. "And a good many of my friends do as well. But even if we didn't, what would it matter? Surely we don't determine truth by popular vote. Couldn't something be true even if no one believed it?"

The consistency of our beliefs and our actions

"One thing at a time," replied Graham. "I know you and your colleagues *say* you believe your explanation, but do you really believe it in the sense that you are willing to live as though it were true? And yes, it does matter. You see, if you don't believe it this way, then your belief is only an academic theory which you aren't really willing to follow. It would be like a person who claimed not to believe in gravity but was not willing to jump out of a third-floor window. She says she believes it, but she really doesn't."

"I get your point. But why do you wonder if I really believe in my own model? I am advocating it, aren't I?"

Graham folded his hands under his chin thoughtfully. "Here's why," he said wryly. "If your evolutionary model is true, then there seems to be no basis for condemning any action at all."

Evolutionary morality: no basis for condemning any act

William was slightly taken aback. "Come again?" he stammered.

"Well," said Graham, "there are certain actions that are abhorrent to all of us. Like rape, stealing, assault and deception. We condemn these regularly."

"And we should!" William responded, raising his voice.

"But if your model is true, how can we?"

"Why can't we?"

"Think of it this way," Graham answered. "Suppose we discovered beings on another planet."

William nodded. "So you're a Trekkie too?" He had often wondered whether extraterrestrials really existed.

"Would rape be wrong for them?" Graham continued.

"It must be. Rape is a terrible thing," William responded.

"But remember, on your model these beings have an entirely different evolutionary history from ours. I ask this question because one philosopher who advocates your evolutionary model, Michael Ruse, uses this very example. His answer to the question is that rape would not necessarily be wrong for other beings on other planets. In his view, although the immorality of rape is a human constant, we cannot thereby think that it would be a constant for other organisms and extraterrestrials."[4]

"Okay, I guess I'd have to agree with that," William replied.

"So would I," said Graham. "On the evolutionary model, we cannot assume that extraterrestrials' morality would be like ours. It all depends on how their particular evolutionary process went."

"Even if that's true," objected William, "what does that have to do with *our* morality?"

"Good question," interrupted Ted. "I think Graham is onto something here. It has everything to do with morality. Suppose these extraterrestrials landed on planet earth and were sufficiently like us that they were able to have sexual relations with us."

"No, thanks!" blurted Ian.

"I know, I know. It doesn't sound appealing. I just said 'if.' My question is, how ought they to act toward us? Suppose they decide to begin raping humans at will. And suppose we complain that rape is wrong and that they should stop. They would have a very ready response. They could simply say, 'Your moral ideas are only a product of your evolutionary process. They are only like your other adaptations. Any other meaning is an illusion. It doesn't affect us.' And if morality is strictly an evolutionary product, they would be right.

"Or suppose they were as superior to us as we are to cattle, and they began using us for food or as laboring animals. What could we possibly tell them on this evolutionary model to show them they are wrong? They have their own system of morality, a product of their own evolutionary development. Why should they adopt human morality?"

"Your point being?" William asked, circling his hands as if to draw a response from Ted.

"My point is that if morality is only an evolutionary product, then raping and killing humans is not really wrong as you previously said. We just have the *conviction*, the *feeling*, that they are wrong. But in that case the extraterrestrials would be fully justified in ignoring our moral sentiments if they so chose. We would have nothing to say to them.

"But the real point that we must not miss here is that on

your model, these acts are no more wrong for us than they are for these extraterrestrials. The fact that we are human does not make an act any more wrong in itself. It just means that we happen to have the *feeling* that it is wrong because of our evolutionary development.

"Now the more important question arises. Why shouldn't we rape, and maim, and steal, and defraud, and do anything else that catches our fancy? We may have a feeling that these acts are wrong. That feeling may even be very strong. But on this view it is simply a biological adaptation inculcated into us over millions of years. It's a feeling, nothing more. There is no reason to regard any act as really right or wrong. In fact, on your evolutionary model it may even be possible to argue that rape is ethically good, because it propagates the species."

William jumped to his feet. "Rape! Good?" he exploded. "Let the record show that I never said it! Nor would I!"

"I'm sure you wouldn't," responded Ted, somewhat taken aback by William's outburst. "But the view you are advocating just might, and that is what is important here. Your evolutionary view has no way of condemning rape, or anything else for that matter, as really wrong. It might even sanction something as awful as rape."

There was silence for a moment as the group digested these latest ideas. Then Francine spoke up. "So we're back to a purely subjective morality?"

"It looks that way," replied Ted. "And my question is, are you willing to live as though these terrible acts aren't really wrong, they just seem so?"

Sitting down, he continued. "This is a critical question to be asked of any viewpoint whatsoever. It's one thing to hold to a belief academically. It's another to genuinely believe it such that we can live it out consistently, and believing the evolutionary explanation means also believing actions such as murder, rape and lying are not genuinely wrong. But William has made it clear that he believes these actions *are* wrong, really objectively wrong."

Suddenly Ian spoke up, eyebrows furrowed. "But surely the fact that William or anyone else does not genuinely believe his own theory does not disprove the theory. I mean, as he said, couldn't it still be true?"

"Good point!" affirmed Ted, "And yes, of course it could, but we must be careful here. First, why should we say it might be true when we have no reason to think it's true and when we ourselves don't even believe it's true, as seen by our actions?

"Second, we must be careful not to contradict ourselves here. You see, we can't have it both ways. If we don't believe this theory, then we are actually saying we don't think it is true. We can't say, 'I don't believe this theory, but it's probably true nonetheless,' without contradicting ourselves. And our earlier point was that by our actions we can often tell what we really believe. If our actions show that we believe certain acts are really objectively wrong, then we are saying that the evolutionary model is not true. In that case we must search for another."

By this time the fire had burned low. Time was moving on. Ted knelt down to push the coals together. All that could be heard was the sound of renewed crackling as the embers stimulated each other to one final outburst of heat and light. For the discussion partners, it was as if the stunning realization of what had just taken place in their small circle was dawning on them all at the same time.

They had all taken their best shot at accounting for objective moral value, and they knew it. All except Ted, that is. The coherence method had failed. The human nature and human need models had similarly proven unsuccessful. A social contract certainly could not account for objective value. And now the evolutionary model had been seen to have critical weaknesses as well.

Could that mean there was no explanation for objective morality? But there had to be, unless they were willing to admit that something existed without an adequate cause. Now there was a bitter pill to swallow indeed. It violated the well-established principle of sufficient reason.

Or could it mean that the explanation for this entity was simply out of reach of human understanding? Unattainable? In which case their best course of action would be to admit it and drop the inquiry. After all, didn't Socrates say that the wisest person was the one who realized the limitations of his knowledge and admitted his ignorance of things that were beyond him?

Somehow, all guessed the others were wondering the same things. The sound of Ted's voice brought them back to reality. "So where does this bring us?" he asked.

"To a dead end!" replied Graham despondently.

"Ah, giving up so soon, are we?"

"You call this soon? I'm beginning to wonder if there is an explanation for objective moral value."

"It does cause one to wonder," agreed William.

Ted sat down and leaned forward intently, and the others fell silent again. "You must all know that there is one more explanation not yet mentioned in our discussions. Before we give up our search, we must hear of it too."

"We're waiting," Graham cut in.

"Ah, but we're out of time."

"I might have known." Graham was having difficulty hiding his frustration.

"But we must hear it," said Ted. "No discussion like ours would be complete without it."

Just then the doorkeeper entered. Hearing Ted's comment, he asked spiritedly, "Then you will be returning next week?"

"I wouldn't miss Ted's explanation for the world!" Graham exclaimed. The others agreed.

"Wonderful!" he replied.

With that they were off to their respective rides. In the car, Ted relaxed and contemplated the discussions of the previous weeks. He thought how all along they had been trying to account for the existence of this entity called objective moral value. Its existence was undeniable. To deny it led to all the harsh contradictions and dead ends they had found in their earlier discussions. To provide a foundation for it was another matter.

Now was his turn. *How will the others take to a God foundation?* he wondered. He knew what he had to do, and the week ahead would be dominated by the task.

11
INTRODUCING GOD
A Christian Theist Foundation

I t was late, and Ted was thinking about what he would say at the next luncheon. He was also trying to figure out how to discover who the mystery host was.

He switched on the local news before retiring for the evening. To his amazement, there on the screen was the doorkeeper. So much for having to find him. He jumped up and turned up the volume. The doorkeeper was speaking.

It didn't take Ted long to realize that he was more than a doorkeeper. He was a judge. In fact, he was the chairman of the Judges Association.

"Incredible!" Ted muttered to himself. He noticed how skillfully the man fielded legal questions concerning case backlogs.

Someone has a lot of explaining to do, he thought. *What else don't I know?*

He quickly caught the judge's name. Suddenly the name of the owner of the big house, the face of the doorkeeper and the fact that he was a judge all came together in his mind. "You! You are the mystery host!" Ted shouted. "Well, have I got some questions for you!"

The next day Ted contacted a colleague in the Law School as well as a lawyer friend. They filled in more details. "Your friend the judge, or should I say doorkeeper," chuckled his colleague, "is from an old-money family. If money can buy it and he wants it, he's got it."

That explains the house and lavish surroundings, the chauf-feured rides, Ted thought to himself.

"I'm telling you," continued the colleague, "what you saw on TV last night is no put-on. This man has a solid legal career behind him. He's highly respected in the legal profession."

I may not have you all figured out, Ted muttered to himself, *but I'm onto you now.*

On the appointed day, the car arrived at its usual time. *I hope today is a day of solutions,* he thought. *We've been at this a long time.*

By the time he arrived at the big house, he had rehearsed his opening line. Sure enough, there was the doorkeeper, carrying out his duties impeccably as usual.

A mystery unraveling

"So you're *more* than a doorkeeper!" Ted blurted out.

Their eyes met, and the doorkeeper gave him a knowing look but said nothing.

He doesn't want to tell me more than he has to, Ted thought to himself. But by this time he was determined to know more. "I think you owe me an explanation. I saw you on the news last night. You're a judge, and an influential one at that. Would you care to expand on that?"

The doorkeeper glanced around nervously to see who else might be listening. Ted pushed ahead with his interrogation. "Who are you? Why are we here? What's this all about? The invitations? The rides? The discussions? The others?" He pointed toward the reception room.

"Wait! Please!" The doorkeeper raised his hands toward Ted and then paused briefly. "Please be patient until the end of the discussion today, and I will tell you who I am. I will answer all your questions. But now, you do realize the others are eagerly waiting for your explanation." He motioned Ted toward the reception room.

Ted was thrust into the midst of the discussion group. They greeted one another. He didn't have to worry about anyone bringing up the issue of the mystery host, because the usual small talk was virtually absent. The others were there for one purpose only. No sooner had the last person entered the room than Graham voiced the question they were all thinking: "So what is your new way of accounting for objective moral value?"

"Rather abrupt, don't you think?" Ted remarked.

"You do have to admit you left us hanging last week."

"Which means you should be fully ready to hear me out now."

"That's an understatement!"

"Actually, my explanation can be summarized in one word."

"Sounds concise," quipped Francine. "And the word is?"

Ted straightened up, paused and looked directly at each person in the circle. "God," he said softly.

"God!" Graham exploded, jumping to his feet. "Did I hear you right? You're going to tell us that somehow God can account for objective moral value?" *God, the foundation of morality*

Ted nodded. "I take it you have a problem with that."

Graham could hardly contain himself. "Oh no! I've got way more than a problem! First of all, I don't even believe in God. I'm an atheist."

"Yes, you've told us that before."

"What's more, I thought we were sticking to reason, to rational explanations, not religious ones. If there's one thing I'm not, it's religious. I can't believe I came all the way down here for this. I suppose the next thing you're going to tell us is that you've got a minister hiding in the closet who you're going to bring out to preach a sermon to us."

The others had never seen Graham express such visceral opposition to a viewpoint. Something about this one had touched a raw nerve.

A wrong reason to rule God out

The room was quiet for a moment. Then Ted spoke again. "Remember, we're all in this search for truth together. And one thing none of us can afford to do is rule out a possible explanation for objective moral value simply because we don't like it, or because it's new to us, or it sounds religious, or it doesn't sound rational enough. None of these make an explanation wrong. In fact, I must say, arbitrarily disregarding a proposed explanation would be the most irrational move of all, one I hope no one in this room would be willing to make.

"If an explanation is inadequate, then that must be shown. We must subject my explanation to the same scrutiny the previous ones have had to undergo."

"This should be fun," said Graham, sitting down and shaking his head ever so slightly.

"It may be," replied Francine, "but I'm still perplexed about one thing."

"And what is that?" asked Ted.

Francine spoke slowly, choosing each word carefully. "It seems that this explanation requires that people believe in God. And don't only religious people hold this belief? I mean, isn't there something to Graham's complaint about not believing?"

Ted raised his hand. "Not so fast. It may be true in one sense that many people *profess* not to believe in God, but there is another side to that story."

"And that is?"

Latent theism

"That given the right circumstances, a much wider group will betray a deep, latent, almost built-in belief in God."

"You're not going to tell me that even though I say I don't believe in God, I really do, are you?" Graham asked skeptically.

"Oh, I'll let you be the judge of that, but answer this question for me: what are the first words out of a person's mouth when he or she goes through a horrifying experience and narrowly escapes death—whether it be a car skidding out of control on the freeway, a plane going down due to engine failure, or something else?"

"I see," responded Francine. "Thank God!"

"That's right. And what does almost every person in the world do when his or her child is struck down with a serious illness and is in the hospital hovering between life and death?"

"Pray."

"I think you're right," affirmed Ted. "And it's responses like these that give rise to expressions like 'There are no atheists in foxholes.' "

"Are you actually saying," pressed Graham, "that everyone believes in God, even the person claiming to be an atheist? Couldn't these responses be nothing more than acts of desperation? Aren't you reading a little much into them?"

"That's possible," replied Ted. "But it's like we said before. It's one thing to say you believe something and another to live out that belief consistently. The professing atheist is not living consistently with his atheism if he responds to crisis by uttering a prayer. What he is showing by his actions is that even he, with all his efforts to do so, has not totally escaped belief in God. Our reactions in a crisis may show our most gut-level beliefs. All I'm saying is that if we were to take people who had called on God or thanked God or gotten angry with God in the midst of a crisis and ask *them* if they believed in God at those times, the number of professing atheists would be very low.

Living beliefs consistently

"It's rather like C. S. Lewis's rats in the closet. He pictures a closet that is home to a number of rats. They're in there, he says, and when you make a sudden, unannounced entry, you see them scurrying off to their hiding places. But if you approach the closet door noisily, giving them plenty of warning, they're gone before the door is opened. They've had time to hide. The point is that the sudden entry didn't *produce* the rats. It only *revealed* them to be there."

Rats in the closet

"And your point is," added Francine, "that many people

have a latent belief in God."

"Exactly, and a sudden, unexpected crisis can reveal it to be there. It doesn't *cause* it. It only reveals it to be there already."

"Hadn't thought about it that way before," Francine commented. "You're also telling us that you don't think most people will have our problem with your view, because most do believe in God at this basic level."

"Precisely," said Ted. "But let's not get sidetracked here. That fact is not overly important for our search. We are simply asking whether God, if one exists, could adequately account for objective moral value."

"Isn't that what we said about my evolutionary foundation?" asked William. "Some believe in evolution and some don't."

"We did say that. And the fact that some don't did not stop us from asking whether an evolutionary process, if one occurred, could account for objective moral value. We saw that it could not."

"Don't remind me!"

"But you'll also remember," said Ted, "we recognized that if it could account for it, then that fact would constitute a strong argument in favor of evolution."

"And I presume you are going to tell us that the same will be true for your God explanation," said Graham, slowly coming out of his skeptic's shell.

A reason to believe God exists

"Right again." Ted smiled. "Let's face it, if no other explanation than God could account for objective value, then wouldn't that be a strong reason for believing he exists? We have to account for this entity in some way. The rational person, the one really seeking truth, will surely accept the one explanation that succeeds in doing so when no others can be found."

Graham shook his head in amazement. "This is bizarre," he muttered. "I know you are telling us this is the rational approach, but with all this talk about God, it sounds to me like we're jumping into religion here with both feet."

Ted smirked ever so slightly. "Still bothering you, is it?"

"It certainly isn't what I expected."

"Maybe you're making unnecessary distinctions."

"Such as?"

"You seem to be implying that the question of God's existence is important to 'religious people,' as you call them, but to no one else."

"Well, isn't that true?"

"Actually, it is a fundamental question for all of us, be- *God's existence:* cause it affects our entire worldview." *important for all*

"World what?" asked Graham.

"Worldview," replied Ted. "A person's worldview is what we call that person's most basic beliefs about what the world and universe are really like. It is one's set of ideas about what ultimate reality is, what humans are, where we came from, what happens to us at death and so on.

"My point is that philosophers have long recognized that the question of God's existence is one of the most basic questions of all time because many of our other beliefs rest on it. The way we decide on this question will directly affect the answers to many worldview questions. For that reason, philosophers have shown great interest in this question, regardless of their religious perspectives. In fact, if you check most introductory textbooks in philosophy, you will find a section dealing directly with the question of God's existence."

Graham leaned back and thought for a moment before speaking. "I can see how philosophical people might be interested in what reasons there may be for believing God does or does not exist."

"Very much so."

"But don't religious people believe in God simply because they want to? Isn't it just part of their religious system?"

"That's a common misconception. Let me speak specif- *Christianity* ically for Christianity, since I'm a Christian. The answer is *entails truth* no, not necessarily. Part of the Christian life is belief in *claims* certain truth claims. One of the most basic is that God exists. Another is that he revealed himself to humankind as a man, Jesus of Nazareth."

"And," jumped in William, "if it can be shown that there is no God, then religious activity becomes . . ." He stopped, searching for words, his hands raised.

"It becomes not merely nonrational, but absolutely irrational," Ted filled in. "Praying to a God that you are convinced does not exist is irrational. For that reason many thoughtful religious people are concerned about what evidence exists for the reliability of their truth claims. If good reasons can be given for believing God exists, then praying to him, thanking him and calling on him are all perfectly reasonable activities."

"So then, what is the difference between philosophical people and religious people? You seem to be blending them together. The way you've described them, both do the same things."

Christianity's philosophical side Ted laughed. "That's what I was saying earlier about you making unnecessary distinctions. Of course there are differences in the intentions and goals between philosophical and religious people. One group seeks intellectual truth, period. The other seeks truth but also desires to know and worship God. But in a sense we are all philosophers so long as we're concerned about truth regarding any fundamental issues like the existence of God. When the religious person seeks reasons for believing God exists, she is involved in the philosophical dimension of her faith."

"So we *are* getting close to religion," Graham said again.

"True," agreed Ted. "We are speaking of matters that are important to people of faith, but that ought not to stop you so long as you are sincerely interested in pursuing truth wherever it leads. If finding an adequate explanation for objective moral value leads us to God, then you as a truth-seeker should be pleased to have discovered that truth."

There was a short silence as each began to realize that the implications of this explanation could be greater than they had first imagined. Eventually William stood up, walked to the table and began serving the others some refreshments. "I think we had better fortify ourselves for this explanation," he declared.

"Right! Time out," called Francine.

After a time Graham spoke up. "So tell us. How could God account for objective moral value?"

"Of course," said Ted. He rose from his chair and began to pace about the room as he continued talking. "We are asking how to account for objective moral value. Another way to put it is to ask what makes it possible for there to be any moral principles that are objective, obligatory and binding even on those who may disagree with them. My explanation begins with God, who is the Creator of the universe and who also is a moral being. In his nature is a sense of right and wrong. It is part of what and who he is. Furthermore, he is immutable. He cannot change to be anything other than what he now is.

God's nature: the moral standard

"I then assert that this moral Creator God infused his moral knowledge into the minds of the people he created."

Human conscience

"Isn't that what we sometimes call our conscience?" Francine asked.

"Exactly. That is a common way of referring to this human moral capacity. My explanation asks, if there is no God, what could provide objective moral value at all?"

"We've already seen that all the explanations put forward so far fail to do so," said Francine.

"Yes, we have. And that's important, since we have covered all the most common nontheistic attempts," replied Ted.

"You mean explanations that do not include God?"

"Right. My point is that it looks as if there is no way of accounting for this entity apart from God. But we could also think of it this way. Suppose there is no God. Then what are we? We are nothing but accidental byproducts of nature who have evolved relatively recently on this tiny planet, lost somewhere in the heart of a hostile and irrational universe. What is more, we're destined to perish as individuals and as a group in a relatively short period of time."

Human beings without God

"Very eloquently put!" exclaimed Francine.

"But don't miss the point here. Given that scenario, what makes beings like us valuable at all? More important, where would this notion of objective moral value that we all have come from in the first place? You see, a purely materialistic universe of space, time, matter and energy that evolved without a moral Creator would be morally indifferent. Good and evil would not exist. Atoms don't have ethics. Molecules don't have morals. There would be no *real, objective* right and wrong. In a world without God, who's to say whose values are right and wrong? Who's to judge Hitler's morals inferior to those of Mother Teresa?[1]

"But suppose we change the scenario and begin where I do, with a moral Creator God who infuses his moral will into our consciences. Then we can account for both the existence of objective moral value and our widespread knowledge of it. It exists because this moral God exists, and we all know about it because he has infused it into our minds."

All were silent for a few seconds. Then Ted sat down. "So here is where we've come," he said. "We've seen that the other commonly tried methods of accounting for objective value don't succeed. None of them can show us why any moral principles should be binding on anyone at all. We've also seen that a purely material universe devoid of God simply has no way of producing real moral value. The concept of morality loses all real meaning in a universe devoid of God."

Then Ted turned to Francine. "You wrote a letter to the university newspaper last year, condemning the university policy on sexual harassment."

"I most certainly did," she said unapologetically.

"And you did not hesitate to condemn certain people and actions as wrong."

"I see you read my letter."

"Yes, I did. But honestly, without God I see nothing that would make your moral principles binding on anyone who disagreed with them. We've examined the nontheistic attempts to account for an objective moral standard. Now here's the problem. We all do, in fact, hold to and reason according to some basic moral principles. Furthermore, we consider these principles right in an objective sense. But these objective principles simply do not exist in the atheistic worldview."

"So what you are telling us," cut in Francine, "is that an atheist cannot hold to these objective moral principles and at the same time live consistently with his or her worldview."

Living consistently with our worldviews

"That is exactly what I'm saying."

Then William voiced the question they were all wondering about. "I suppose these are fighting words to Graham here and his atheist friends? After all, what atheist is going to admit he has given up any notion of objective right and wrong?"

Ted chuckled. "You may be surprised," he said. "More than a few well-known atheists have realized this consequence of their atheism and admitted they have no basis for objective right and wrong."

William sucked in a hard breath. "That's unbelievable," he whispered.

"Maybe so, but J. L. Mackie, one of the greatest atheists of recent times, admitted that moral value is most unlikely to have arisen without an all-powerful God to ground it. He wrote that if there really is objective value, it would make God's existence more probable than if there weren't. He said this is a defensible argument from morality to the existence of God."[2]

"But he was an atheist!"

"True. Which is why he also rejected the notion of objective moral value. He had to. He recognized that if there was no God, then neither could there be any objective value. He adopted the evolutionary model and believed that we all have the feeling, the sense, that there is objective value but that this is only a feeling developed over a long evolutionary process. There is no objective basis for our moral sense.

"But, as we've seen, that evolutionary foundation fails under close scrutiny. Not only does it leave us unable to condemn any act as genuinely wrong, but it cannot account for many of the moral convictions we humans have."

"Didn't Bertrand Russell also reject objective moral value?" asked William.

"Another good example," affirmed Ted.

"He was an atheist, wasn't he?"

"You might say that," joked Ted. "He did write the book entitled *Why I Am Not a Christian* and was well known for his atheism. But notice, he also contended that with God out of the picture, no other objective standard for morality, which he called 'The Good,' could be found. As he put it, when we try to be definite as to what we mean when we say this or that is 'The Good,' we find ourselves in very great difficulty."

"You sound like you've got it memorized."

"I do—that one statement anyway. It's a well-known one, which he wrote in 1935 in his work entitled *Religion and Science*. He believed no evidence existed for any other moral standard. He then concluded that we are left with a purely subjective morality and argued extensively for it."[3]

"So these atheists were consistent," mused William.

"Yes they were," replied Ted. "You have to give them that, and in my opinion they were correct in linking God to objective moral value. I mean, ask yourself: if there is no God, why wouldn't all our subjectivism be true? How could there be any objective value?

"The Russian writer Fyodor Dostoyevsky recognized this link and wrote the now famous saying 'If there is no God, all things are permitted.' "[4]

With that Ted walked over to the fire and added a log. All watched in silence as the fire grew, throwing shadows that danced along the wall. As Graham watched those changing shadows, he couldn't help realizing how much like them he was becoming. There had been a time when he was firm in his opinions, he thought to himself. He had always prided himself in his intellectual confidence. But one by one his viewpoints were being found inadequate. They simply could not withstand careful scrutiny.

And now, to his chagrin, he was faced with the possibility that God was the only adequate explanation for objective moral value. He had to admit that God did appear to account for both the existence and the widespread knowledge of objective value. Could it be that this was true? The most biting part was that if so, he knew he would either have to accept this explanation and reject the others or else live inconsistently and irrationally. What a choice! What a dilemma!

But then he brightened. The group still had not subjected Ted's explanation to scrutiny. Surely there were hard questions to ask of it, just as there had been of the others.

Suddenly Graham was jerked from his mental detour by the sound of Francine's voice. "I take it you will entertain questions on your explanation? After all, we've all been interrogated."

"Hey, I believe in fairness. It's a basic moral virtue, universally recognized. Fire away!"

"But ladies and gentlemen," interrupted William, "I think first we should interrogate that dessert table. It will be awhile before I see a spread like this again."

There was immediate consensus on William's suggestion, and they moved toward the table.

12
OBJECTING TO GOD

Obstacles to Believing in the God Hypothesis

When their appetites were satisfied, William observed, "This may be the last time we'll enjoy lunch together for a while. This is the last of the attempts at finding a foundation for morality."

"Hey!" cut in Francine. "We're not over yet. Don't read the eulogy on these discussions until we've had a chance to ask Ted a few questions. For starters, Ted, there is one thing bothering me about your explanation."

"Only one?"

"Sorry to disappoint you, but I'm sure the others will have *The atheist's* more. It still seems that your God explanation leaves out the *dilemma* person who doesn't believe in God. Even if an atheist were convinced by your arguments, how could he or she adopt your model? Doesn't it assume something that atheists already deny?"

"No," replied Ted, "except in a purely scientific sense."

"Oh, now we're into science!" said a skeptical Graham.

Scientific Christianity "We have been all along, only we haven't been using the terminology. Doesn't science attempt to explain a certain set of data by proposing a hypothesis and then analyzing it carefully to see if it succeeds as an explanation?"

"Yes."

"Well, that's what we've been doing too. The datum we've been trying to explain is objective moral value. It's there. We've agreed we can't deny it. You've all proposed your explanations, or should we say your hypotheses, and we've analyzed them. Now I'm proposing mine."

Francine pondered his words momentarily. "And you would ask the atheist to examine God as a hypothesis? That doesn't sound like the way I've heard people talk about God."

"True, but there is nothing demeaning about it. We're simply trying to determine whether or not a moral Creator could adequately explain objective value."

"But don't you think the atheist will find this hypothesis difficult to swallow?"

"Possibly, but the search for truth does not concern itself with making truth palatable, only with making it known. You see, we cannot deny or ignore an explanation simply because it conflicts with something else we now believe. Not if we're really wanting to get at truth. That would be an ostrich mentality. Putting your head in the sand like that would eliminate your chances of ever learning new truth. If there are good reasons for believing a new idea, then maybe we need to rethink our old ones."

"And you're telling us to follow this procedure for the question 'Does God exist?' "

An argument for God's existence "Precisely. Our viewpoint on this question likewise has to be arrived at by examining the reasons both for and against. What I have presented here is one reason in favor of God's existence. A particular entity which we all agree exists, namely, objective moral value, cannot be accounted for in any other way than by a moral Creator God. That should lead the honest observer nearer to the conclusion that there is such a God."

"You sure have a way with words," Graham quipped. "Now you're shifting the responsibility onto the atheist."

"No more than we did in our look at the evolutionary model, if you'll recall. We said then that if it turned out to be a good explanation for objective moral value, a necessary implication would be that an evolutionary process would become much more likely.

"You see, if the atheist refuses even to examine any reasons for the idea that God exists, he has put his head in the sand. He has placed himself out of reach of ever learning new truth again."

Francine nodded. "So you're saying that the atheist is not really left out of this model?"

"Not at all. It's just that if he finds my moral Creator model convincing, he will have to rethink his atheism. My model actually becomes a reason for believing God exists."

"I can see that!" sputtered Graham.

"But if our atheist friend is genuinely concerned with finding truth, then this shouldn't bother him. In fact he should be willing, even pleased, to examine this new piece of evidence. If it points him to a different conclusion from the one he now holds, so be it. He will have just discovered a truth he didn't know before. He is the winner for it."

"Oh, this is good!" replied Graham, his words dripping with sarcasm. "Now we've turned our atheist into a winner."

"Don't you agree that a person who discovers a significant truth for the first time is a winner for it?"

Graham shook his head but said nothing.

"We still haven't mentioned the critical problem with your model," said Francine.

"Which is?"

"Don't they call it the Euthyphro problem?"[1]

"Ah yes," Ted responded with an affirming nod. "That is an important objection. I see you've been reading your Plato lately."

The Euthyphro problem

"Hold on a minute," cut in Graham. "The what problem?"

"It is a problem first raised in one of Plato's dialogues called the *Euthyphro,*" said Ted. "Explain it for us, Francine. You raised it."

"Well," she began, "Ted is telling us that the source of all judgments of good and bad is God. It all goes back to him. If God says something is good, then it is, and vice versa."

"Uh-huh." Ted was nodding cautiously. "So what's the problem?"

"The problem is figuring out just *how* God can be the source of objective moral value. There are only two options in the matter. Either an action is good because God commands it, or he commands it because it is good."

"Not so fast!" Graham protested, mulling these thoughts over momentarily. "Just these two? You're sure about that?"

"What else could there be?"

"Okay then," replied Graham. "What's the problem with these two options?"

"The problem," answered Francine, "is that neither of them can be true. Suppose the first one were correct: actions are good strictly because God commands them."

"What's the problem with that?" pressed Graham.

The problem of arbitrary morality

"That option cannot be true," replied Francine, "because the simple act of commanding or forbidding an action does not in itself make any action good or bad. That's true whether it is God or anyone else doing the commanding."

"Just a minute," interjected Graham. "Why not?"

"Think about it. If that were the only reason we had for calling an action right or wrong, then it would make right and wrong arbitrary."

"Which means?"

"It means there would be no reason for the choice of one act being better than another. It's whatever the one commanding wants, and that's that. It would be no different from a bully who tells you something is right because he says so and that's all there is to it. You'd better go along with him or else. There is really no reason for it to be right. He just decided to call it right and is big enough to force his will on a weaker person."

Ted leaned forward. "You're saying God is like a bully?"

"Sorry. Bad analogy. No offense. My only point is that if something is right strictly because God says it is, according to the first option, there would be nothing that would make God's commands *right*. Certainly the fact that he commanded them wouldn't do it. Nor would the fact that he is bigger than us and able to impose his will on us. Right and wrong would be arbitrary. That is really the fundamental problem with this first option. God could simply have called anything good or bad. Rape. Murder. Stealing. Assault."

"Okay, okay! I've got your point," Graham exclaimed. "So then how do we escape this arbitrariness? What would we need for God's commands to be truly good?"

"I thought you'd never ask," Francine quipped. "If an act is to be genuinely right or wrong, there must be a standard of goodness. All actions could then be measured against this standard. Those that conform to it are good. Those that don't are bad. But if there is no standard, we have lost our basis for calling anything good or bad in any objective sense. The fact that something is commanded, in and of itself, cannot make any act right or wrong." *The need for a moral standard*

Graham paused, then collected his thoughts. "So the first option is inadequate. It won't do to say an action is good because God commands it?"

"Afraid so."

"But you mentioned two options."

"Yes," said Francine. "There is another way that some theists believe God could be the source of objective moral standards, and that is to say that he commands an action because it is good."

"Interesting," Graham mused. "That would escape the arbitrariness problem."

184

Can We Be Good
Without God?

*The question of
God's moral
standard*

"Yes, it would," replied Francine, "but it raises a different one. You see, if God commands something because it is good, we must ask what makes it good. And as we've just seen, for anything to be truly good, there must be some standard of goodness to which the thing conforms. Otherwise we're back to an arbitrary command.

"But this means that even for God, if he is commanding something *because it is good,* then there must be a standard of goodness to which he conforms.

"What's more, for you and me to *know* that God, or anything else, is good, we must have prior knowledge of what good and evil are. That same standard must be in our minds. Then if we see God or his commands conforming to that standard, we can know he is good. But without that prior knowledge, how can I know that even God is good?"

"That's a mouthful!" said Graham, shaking his head. "What you're saying is that for goodness to exist at all, there must be a standard of goodness."

"Right."

"And for God to be good, he must conform to this standard."

"Yes."

"And for us to know God is good, we must have knowledge of this standard in our minds ahead of time."

"Exactly!" exclaimed Francine.

Graham paused thoughtfully. "Well, then, am I missing something? Where's the problem?"

"The problem is—and here's the crunch—that God is no longer the source of good. He simply conforms to it. The standard of goodness exists independent of him."

"Ooh!" Graham winced. "There went the second option."

Francine nodded. "It does seem that either option leaves us unable to account for objective moral value by referring to God." She leaned back and raised both hands into the air as if to invite a response. *However,* she thought to herself, *what is there to say? The Euthyphro objection seems unanswerable.*

Ted looked over at Francine. "Very well stated. I always appreciate a strong advocate of any position. Quite convinced by it, aren't you?"

"Shouldn't I be?" She smiled and raised her eyebrows.

"Now that is what we have to find out," responded Ted. "There was a time when I was too, but no longer."

"I didn't expect you to like it," Francine said. "After all, it works havoc on your God model. But can you find something wrong with it? That's the important question. It looks airtight to me."

"I'm sure it does, but your objections to the two options miss an important distinction."

"Which is?"

"They confuse the categories of knowing and being."

"Come again?"

Knowing versus being

"It's one thing for something to be, or to exist. It's an entirely different thing for me to *know* it exists. *Being*—that is, existing—and *knowing* are two distinct categories."

"Of course. But how have I confused these two?" Francine was perplexed.

"Let's think carefully about what you just said," Ted continued. "You have argued that for anything to be good, including God or Jesus, or one of their commands, or any action for that matter, there must be a standard of goodness."

"Yes, I have."

"And for me to recognize good, whether in God or anywhere else, I must know about this standard."

"What is this, an exercise in communication?"

"As a matter of fact, it sometimes does help to have the hearer repeat back to the speaker what she just said in his own words. It guarantees he has caught the point as intended."

"Well, you've heard me well so far."

"But you also said this standard had to be independent of God."

"Precisely. Otherwise there would be no good or bad for

him."

"And that is where the confusion is."

"Where?"

"You see, knowing that this standard of goodness exists and applies to God tends to make us also assume that it must be independent of him, different from him. But that is not necessarily so. It is true that our *knowledge* of it must come before we can apply it back to God. But as to its *existence,* it could have existed in God before we knew about it. It could have derived from God. And, in fact, that is exactly what I am arguing: that, as you say, there must be a standard and we must know about it, but that God himself is the standard.

"God infuses knowledge of this standard into our minds. This gives us knowledge of goodness, or we could say moral knowledge. This knowledge of goodness enables us to recognize good when we see it, whether in God, in Jesus or anywhere else. The point is that we knew good and evil before we could recognize it in God or anywhere else, but it existed in God prior to our knowledge of it."

Francine shook her head. "Let me get this straight. You're arguing that God is the standard that we come to know about and then apply back to him?"

"Exactly. And we apply this same standard to all other actions as well."

"So you're admitting we need a prior knowledge of good?"

"Yes, I am. And we have it. As a matter of fact, that is what we've been calling objective moral value, and it's firmly rooted in our minds. We've seen that throughout our discussion. That standard of good is the fact that no one can deny."

"So," said Francine, "you are going with my second option: God commands things because they are good."

"Yes I am, and good actions are good because they conform to an objective standard of goodness. But," Ted said, pausing briefly, "the difference is that this standard of goodness is not independent of God, as you say. It is rooted in his nature, his character. And that is also why there is nothing arbitrary about God's value system. Arbitrary would mean randomly picking and choosing this or that moral principle with no reason. That is not true of God. There is a reason his moral values are what they are, and that is because he is what he is. They are rooted in his very nature."

"Hmm," Francine mused quietly. "So God himself is the standard. Moral values are rooted in his nature, and there is nothing arbitrary about it." She had to admit she was intrigued by this response to her objection. But there did seem to be one critical weakness. "Astute response," she said. "It does open up another question, however."

"Which is?"

"What makes God's nature good? You have said that God's nature is the ultimate standard of right and wrong."

The goodness of God's nature

"Yes."

"But I'm not sure that really answers the question. Don't we need to push this one step further and ask what makes God's nature itself good? I know you say it is not arbitrary, but there still seems to be something arbitrary about saying God's nature is simply good and that's that. What if his nature were different? I imagine you would still want to call it good. It still seems to be arbitrary to take God's nature, whatever it happens to be, and say it's good and that's that."

"Relentless, aren't you? Let's get one thing straight. I'm not saying God's nature is simply good and that's that. But more about that later. You ask what if God's nature were different. Well, the first thing to remember about God's nature is that it could not be different from what it is. You see, God is not only eternal, he is also immutable, unchanging. That means that he is what he is and could not be different."

"That sounds like a cop-out!" Francine exclaimed. "I'm tempted to say, 'How convenient!' How can you just say that?"

"Hey! Hey! Remember, we are all putting forth our views, or models as we've been calling them, as hypotheses to be tested. We're trying to determine which view will best account for the existence of objective moral value. My model is the Christian moral Creator God, and the Christian concept of God has always been that he is not only eternal but also immutable. It's in the Scriptures and in any theological text worth reading as well. Surely you're not opposed to it because it works, because it helps to avoid a problem?"

Francine nodded but remained silent.

"I'm simply asking whether or not the Christian God can account for the objective moral value that none of us can deny. If he can, that's one more reason for believing he actually exists."

Francine sat thoughtfully but said nothing, so Ted continued.

"Another point needs to be made here. We may be raising a problem that doesn't exist."

"It sure seems real to me."

"But is it? If we think about this carefully, we'll see that there really can be no question about the goodness of God's nature."

"And why would you say that?" Francine demanded.

Moral standards: tested by what they approve

"Because I see what it has produced."

"And what is that?"

"The moral values that we've been speaking of all along."

"You're losing me. Come again?"

"Sure. Let's get your objection straight. You are saying that even if objective moral values are rooted in God's nature, there is still the question whether God himself is good."

"Exactly!"

"Well now, let me ask you this. On what basis would you decide that any moral standard is good?"

"Oh, I see," responded Francine. "You would look to see what kinds of actions it approves, the kinds of moral judgments it makes."

"Precisely. You would look at what it approves of."

"But isn't there something odd about that?" Francine persisted. "We're now judging the standard by the actions it approves. Isn't it supposed to be the other way around? I thought the standard was there to judge the actions as good or bad."

"Great observation, and yes, it looks unusual. What it shows us, however, is that we humans have a certain amount of built-in moral knowledge. It's just there, and it allows us to judge certain moral standards or guidelines as illegitimate if they approve actions that we all know to be immoral.

"You see, throughout our entire discussion we've recognized that certain acts are good and others bad."

"Right."

"That is what we *know*, even if we can't figure out how we know it or what makes them good or bad. We know that truth, honesty, fairness and respect for human life are good and their opposites are bad. In fact, if you'll recall, that's what the atheist with his coherence model directed us to do: simply start with moral truisms like these, which, he said, we all know to be true, even if we don't know how."

"Uh-huh."

"But notice something. Once we've agreed these values are good, we have no choice but to regard any standard that denounces them as an immoral standard. One that approves them is thereby seen to be a good standard. Remember, this standard is the source and standard of all that we already know to be good. There is no question of its goodness if it approves of what we already know to be good and disapproves of what we know is not."

"Let me get this straight," Francine pressed. "Are you saying that God is good because the values he produces are good?"

"Close, but not quite," Ted answered. "The fact that he produced these values is not what *makes* him good. Rather, that is what *shows* him to be good. Any moral standard that approves of good actions *shows itself* to be good. It's one thing for him to be good, quite another for us to *know* he is good. And that is the answer to your question of how we know God's nature is good. We know it because the values he produced and conforms to are good."

Francine paused briefly, then responded. "Okay, I'll grant you that if God's nature judges these good actions to be good, then he must be good. But," she continued, "aren't we missing something here?"

"Such as?"

"What you've shown is how we *know* God's nature is good. You still haven't told us *why* it is good. What makes it good? How did it come to be a good nature? Especially with no other standard pronouncing God to be good. I thought we had agreed that without a moral standard, nothing can be truly good."

God's own moral standard

"Yes, I did. I'll answer your question about God needing a standard to be good as long as you'll admit that it is largely an academic matter by now, since we've already, both of us, admitted that we know God is good."

"Call it academic if you want . . ."

"I will because it is. But let's ask, if you wish, how God can be good with no superior standard judging him to be good. I agree it sounds odd to our ears, because any moral judgment we make must be measured by some standard. However, look at it this way. Suppose you insist that there must be another higher standard that judges God's nature to be good. I would then have to ask you what makes this other standard good, and you would have to appeal to a still higher one. But then that higher standard will require a still higher one to judge it. We could go on and on forever, but if every standard we appeal to must itself be judged by a still higher one, then there would be no final, ultimate standard.

"But if no final standard exists, then why should we think any of the other lesser standards are good? They would all merely be grounded in other standards which could not stand on their own. Every standard we ever appeal to would depend on yet another standard for its own goodness. And if there never is an independent, final standard that gives a basis to all the others, it means all the standards we have are ultimately groundless and give no reliable statement of what is good and evil."

"That's deep!" Graham grimaced.

"And remember what we all saw earlier," Ted continued. "For any real right and wrong to exist in the world, there must be a final standard that ultimately defines good for us. And since we all know that there is real right and wrong, we must conclude that there is a final standard somewhere. No matter what this standard is, it will be open to the criticism you are leveling against God—namely, that no other standard judges it to be good. But since some final standard somewhere is necessary to determine what good and evil are, it doesn't count as an objection against God to say that he is the final standard."

Ted paused and leaned back in his chair. "Let me be very clear here. I am arguing only that the God hypothesis works. If goodness is a part of God's essential nature, then God is an adequate foundation for objective moral standards. The Euthyphro objection fails to disprove it.

"But there is more to say about why the Christian God ought to be regarded as this standard. All along I've been referring to him as a moral Creator God, and the fact that he is the Creator and source of all things except himself is an integral part of the Christian concept of God. Now we've all agreed that good and evil must go back to some standard. That is unavoidable. My contention is that the most logical, consistent place to take it back to is the source of all things. Apart from him there is no standard—or anything else, for that matter.

"Since there has to be a standard somewhere which ultimately defines good and evil, what is the problem with God being that standard? We must remember that this does not mean that just anything at all could have been good or evil. Quite the contrary, since God is immutable. He is what he is and could never change. Therefore good and evil are what they are and could never change.

"In my judgment, this provides the basis we need to account for the existence of real right and wrong."

The room was quiet as Ted's foundation sank in.

"Well, you certainly have given us something to think about," Francine said at last.

Graham the atheist, William the evolutionist and Ian the humanist were also contemplating Ted's conclusion. Long-held views would have to be reexamined in the light of this discussion—and all those that had preceded it.

Suddenly the silence was broken by the opening of the door. The doorkeeper stepped in. "Hello, everyone."

"Why, hello!" returned William.

"I guess I have some explaining to do."

William was nonplused. "You? Some explaining? About what?"

"You see, I am the one who invited you here."

A stunned silence spread through the room. "I don't believe this!" muttered Graham.

A judge who judges

Then Ted spoke up. "It's true. I accidentally discovered, only this week, that our host is a judge. He promised to answer our questions."

"A judge?" exclaimed William.

"I'm afraid so," replied the doorkeeper.

"But these meetings," William continued. "Why? What is the purpose?"

"I've been thinking about that," spoke up Ted, "and I have an idea. I suspect that our host, being a judge, has a natural professional curiosity about morality. Am I right, Judge?"

The doorkeeper stepped forward. All eyes were fixed on him. "First of all, I want to thank you for coming here faithfully. Second, I have been monitoring your conversations, and I apologize for doing that without asking you first. However, only I have heard them, and it seemed the best way to achieve my goals, even if it was a bit underhanded.

"I chose this method because I didn't want to influence the course of the discussion. I too am used to hearing evidence presented verbally and listening to all sides of the story. I didn't want to read only one side of this discussion in some textbook."

"I'm less concerned with your eavesdropping on us than with why we're here," said Ian.

"I'm getting to that. Ted is right. It is for professional reasons, but there are also personal motives. Strong ones!" the judge emphasized.

The shock of his announcement was over, and the five sat listening as the judge calmly explained himself. "I'm sure you've noticed I am the only person you see around here."

Ted nodded.

"I have a daughter who is estranged. She tours with a modern dance company and will have nothing to do with me. My other child, a son, seemed at first to be following the lifestyle I had hoped for him: an M.B.A., then the beginnings of a successful investment banking career. Then cocaine and embezzlement charges shattered our illusions."

Ted grimaced. "I'm sorry."

The judge went on. "My wife and I are still married, but recently she decided to go for an extended solo trip to Europe. She said to give her a call when I got my life in order. So you can see, I'm not very good at keeping people around me—another reason I wanted you to debate the issues without my being present.

"And here I am at this point in my life wondering whether there is any point to it all."

"But," cut in Ted, "you said there were also professional reasons for getting us together?"

"Yes," replied the judge. "There are." He paused, and a look of anguish settled in his eyes. "Have you ever wondered what it's like to send a person to jail for ten years, or twenty-five?" *A judge needs a foundation for judging*

No one spoke, so he continued. "Think of it: ten years out of someone's life because of a decision *you* made, sometimes with the help of a jury."

"That would be tough," Graham murmured.

"It's tough all right, at the best of times," continued the judge, "but there's something that has made it especially brutal for me."

"What's that?" Graham blurted out.

"The question you've all been debating. What if there actually is no real, objective right and wrong? Oh, I know some in my profession tell me to ignore questions of morality and just interpret and enforce the law as it stands. But think about it. If there really is no true right and wrong, what is our reason for punishing criminals? For destroying their lives for ten or twenty years? It boils down to their having done something we do not like. We decide arbitrarily to send them to prison, and we can't even say that what they've done to deserve it is truly wrong!

"You see, it's one thing to punish someone if you really believe they've done wrong. I can handle that. But what I can't handle is the thought of destroying another human being's life if I'm not even sure they did wrong. And of course, if there is no real, objective right and wrong, then whatever they've done, however unpalatable I find it, is not wrong. So what business do I have sending them to jail for it?

"Sleeping at night has not been easy lately, and that was my reason for getting you together: to get some answers to some questions like, What's it all about? Is there any real moral right and wrong, or do we just make it up as we go along? And what part does God have to play in any of this?"

"You certainly go for the easy ones, don't you?" Graham chuckled. "Actually, these are as fundamental as they come. Most people avoid these kinds of questions."

"Not when you're where I am," responded the judge. "Obviously I couldn't control the topic of conversation, so I decided to choose a number of guests with different worldviews."

"But how did you choose us?" said Francine.

"That was the easy part. I just phoned a few universities and associations and asked for the names of the best spokespeople on certain viewpoints for a future debate. That's how I got each of your names."

"And you've no doubt noticed," spoke up Graham, "that

we have debated two questions really. First, are there objective moral standards? Second, if so, how do we explain
them? What is their foundation? And then we asked whether or not God was necessary to explain them. Can there be
any true moral goodness without God?"

"Yes, I've noticed. And I can see that if there is no objective morality, I have no business judging my son's behavior as good or bad. Or my daughter's, or anyone who stands
in my court convicted of any crime whatsoever. All I can do
is indicate my preferences."

"Exactly!" replied Ted.

"I also see that if there *are* objective moral standards, they
must be explained some way. Believe me, I've listened very
closely to all of your explanations. I've also paid close attention to how each stands up under scrutiny. That is my job,
you know."

"We know," said Ted. "So now you have a decision to *Decision time*
make. I'm sure you know that the way you make it will
fundamentally affect the kind of person you become."

The judge seemed to be drifting off in thought. "Yes," he
whispered almost to himself. "Decision time."

Wanting to inject a little levity, Francine spoke up. "I'll tell
you what, Judge. We'll leave you with our recipe for thinking
about objective morality if you give me the recipe for that
chicken dish over there."

"I want the one for that cheesecake last week," spoke up
William. "It's definitely a recipe that has evolved to perfec-
tion." They all laughed.

"And I'd like a glass of that punch," said Ian, "to quench
my thirst and to raise a toast to our host, the judge." Having
filled his glass, he laughed and raised it high. "To all of you,
and to challenging dialogue!"

"To the truth!" said the judge.

Their glasses clinked. As they caught one another's gaze,
they knew they would never be the same.

Notes

Chapter 1: What's at Stake?

[1]For a fuller explanation and defense of secular humanism, see Paul Kurtz, *In Defense of Secular Humanism* (Buffalo, N.Y.: Prometheus, 1983).

[2]This statement by Francine represents what is usually known as moral noncognitivism. Its thesis is that moral judgments are *not* making truth claims, as you would if you said, "There are five people in this room." Rather, moral judgments merely express the emotions or attitude of the speaker. For that reason a distinction has been made within noncognitivism between the emotive theory and the attitude theory. I will not be concerned with which type of noncognitivist Francine might be. What is important is only that in her view there are no absolute or objective moral principles. Thus when she makes a moral statement, she merely expresses her emotions or attitude about something. Furthermore, another person's attitude toward the issue is just as worthwhile as hers.

[3]This argument is made more fully by Peter Kreeft, *Between Heaven and Hell* (Downers Grove, Ill.: InterVarsity Press, 1982), pp. 31-32.

[4]For a further treatment of ethical relativism, see the collection of articles *Relativism: Interpretation and Confrontation*, ed. Michael Krausz (Notre Dame, Ind.: University of Notre Dame Press, 1989). See also Clifford Geertz, "Anti Anti-relativism," *American Anthropologist* 86 (1984): 263-78.

[5]This is the explanation and illustration of the subjectivity of values given by Bertrand Russell. He advocated this doctrine in *Religion and Science* (Oxford: Oxford University Press, 1935), pp. 237-43. Another proponent is J. L. Mackie, *Ethics: Inventing Right and Wrong* (New York: Penguin, 1977), pp. 15-48. For a similar explanation but from a critic's perspective, see Donald Davidson, "The Myth of the Subjective," in *Relativism: Interpretation and Confrontation*, ed. Michael Krausz (Notre Dame, Ind.: University of Notre Dame Press, 1989), pp. 159-72. Another critic of the subjective view is A. R. C. Duncan, *Moral Philosophy* (Toronto: CBC Enterprises, 1965), pp. 37-48. In addition, James Rachels offers a very readable explanation of ethical subjectivism in *The Elements of Moral Philosophy* (New York: McGraw-Hill, 1986), pp. 30-43.

⁶This view is explained and advocated in Duncan, *Moral Philosophy*, pp. 49-60. Furthermore, this is the view held by Plato; see *The Republic*, trans. F. M. Cornford (Oxford: Oxford University Press, 1941). For further reading see Catherine Elgin's article "The Relative Fact and the Objectivity of Value," in *Relativism: Interpretation and Confrontation*, ed. Michael Krausz (Notre Dame, Ind.: University of Notre Dame Press, 1989), pp. 86-98.

Chapter 2: What If Morality Were Subjective?
¹See Mark B. Woodhouse, *A Preface to Philosophy*, 4th ed. (Belmont, Calif.: Wadsworth, 1990), pp. 4-5, for a broader explanation of various relationships between ideas. His examples are particularly helpful.
²Of course someone could disagree that we know we are responsible for our actions, but all I'm doing here is showing how this kind of argument works. It's called a reductio ad absurdum argument and is explained in most logic textbooks. A good explanation is found in Brooke Noel Moore and Richard Parker, *Critical Thinking*, 3rd ed. (Palo Alto, Calif.: Mayfield, 1992), pp. 226-27.

Chapter 3: Subjective Morality Found Wanting
¹See chapters one and two for a full discussion of the meaning of these four terms. There I have included definitions, explanations and illustrations, as well as notes for further reading.
²I have found James Rachels's chapter on cultural relativism in *The Elements of Moral Philosophy* (2nd ed. [New York: McGraw-Hill, 1986], pp. 30-43) to be especially helpful in identifying consequences of subjective ethics that are either absurd or unacceptable. A. C. Ewing also sets out some unacceptable consequences of subjective ethics in *The Definition of Good* (New York: Macmillan, 1947), pp. 4-35. In the same essay he examines the case for the subjectivity of ethics and finds it wanting. The case for the subjectivity of ethics is made by J. L. Mackie, *Ethics: Inventing Right and Wrong* (New York: Penguin, 1977), pp. 15-49, and also by Bertrand Russell, *Religion and Science* (New York: Holt, 1935), pp. 229-38.

Chapter 4: Why Morality Must Be Objective
¹David Hume became so convinced of this he argued that the only acceptable viewpoint on any issue of fundamental importance was a thoroughgoing skepticism. In his *Dialogues of Natural Religion*, ed. Norman Kemp Smith (London: Macmillan, 1947), pp. 186-87, he contended that in a dispute every opponent triumphs in showing up the weaknesses in his opponent's position. This, however, demonstrates only that the real winners are skeptics who attempt to defend no view of their own but only criticize others' views. I find this approach to be inadequate, since every person must, implicitly or explicitly, adopt the tenets of some worldview. No one can consistently live like a skeptic. It is still true, however, that criticizing a view is usually easier than defending one.
²See chapter one for a full explanation of objective moral value. There I have defined and illustrated it as well as contrasted it with a subjective understanding of morality.
³Of course someone could argue that our belief that an objective moral standard exists could be mistaken and that therefore the fact that we believe it is there really proves nothing. I do not believe this argument can be so easily set aside, however, and in chapter ten I address this objection specifically. I argue that we cannot have it both ways without contradicting ourselves. We cannot, by our actions, demonstrate that we believe X exists and at the same time argue that X probably does not exist. If we live according to a theory, we thereby show that we believe it. If we believe it, by definition we think it is true. Therefore to assert that

we do not think it is true even while living as though it is is to contradict ourselves. To say it another way: if by our actions we show that we believe that objective moral value exists, then we have rejected the theory that it does *not* exist.

⁴See Brooke Noel Moore and Richard Parker, *Critical Thinking*, 3rd ed. (Palo Alto, Calif.: Mayfield, 1992), pp. 65-70, 257-59, for a helpful explanation of contradictory claims.

⁵C. S. Lewis employs this same illustration (how people argue) in *Mere Christianity* (New York: Macmillan, 1952), pp. 17-21. Here he advances his own argument that an objective moral standard exists which all humans recognize, appeal to and expect others to know about.

⁶I stress this fact because occasionally one hears it argued that the fact that people do not always live according to the principles of fairness, decency, respect for human life and so forth proves that these principles cannot exist in any objective sense. It does nothing of the sort. That conclusion does not follow from this premise.

Chapter 5: Hey, I Object!

¹This objection—that objective moral value does not exist and that the moral sense people have of it is merely an instinct for survival—is part of the evolutionary objection, which will be treated more fully in chapter ten. Here I am simply arguing that instincts are fundamentally different from what we call our moral sense. C. S. Lewis responds to this objection in similar fashion in *Mere Christianity* (New York: Macmillan, 1952), pp. 21-24.

²For a treatment of these and other specific questions concerning a single set of objective moral principles, see Gilbert Harman, "Is There a Single True Morality?" in *Morality, Reason and Truth: New Essays on the Foundations of Ethics*, ed. David Copp and David Zimmerman (Lanham, Md.: Rowman & Allanheld, 1984), pp. 27-48.

³This is Lewis's term (*Mere Christianity*, p. 24).

⁴This is the procedure employed by Lewis (ibid., pp. 24-26).

Chapter 6: But Don't Different Cultures Have Different Moral Practices?

¹This is a common objection to the existence of one true objective moral standard. For further reading on the topic generally, see William Graham Sumner, *Folkways* (New York: Ginn, 1902), especially chapters 1-3. Sumner argues that there is no one set of objective moral values. He makes his case primarily by marshaling a large number of examples of different moral practices in various societies. We cannot discover the origin of moral practices, he says, but they probably represent the various ways people have struggled to survive. For the reasons I outline in this chapter, I find this argument uncompelling. There are better ways to account for differences in moral practices, especially in light of the widespread fundamental similarities. See also Brimal Krishna Matilal, "Ethical Relativism and Confrontation of Cultures," in *Relativism: Interpretation and Confrontation*, ed. Michael Krausz (Notre Dame, Ind.: University of Notre Dame Press, 1989), pp. 339-62; also Gilbert Harman, "Is There a Single True Morality?" in *Morality, Reason and Truth: New Essays on the Foundations of Ethics*, ed. David Copp and David Zimmerman (Lanham, Md.: Rowman & Allanheld, 1984), pp. 27-84. C. S. Lewis also offers a small but helpful treatment of this question in *Mere Christianity* (New York: Macmillan, 1952), pp. 19-20. Robert Ashmore also includes an insightful discussion of the cultural challenge to the objectivity of moral value in *Building a Moral System* (Englewood Cliffs, N.J.: Prentice-Hall, 1987), pp. 41-48. Ashmore challenges the claim that moral values in different communities are *fundamentally* different.

²This document can be found in *International Human Rights Instruments of the United Nations, 1948-1982* (Pleasantville, N.Y.: UNIFO Publishers, 1983), pp. 57, 117. It is also recorded in the appendix of Ashmore, *Building a Moral System*, pp. 163-66

[3]C. S. Lewis, *The Abolition of Man* (New York: Macmillan, 1955), pp. 95-121.

[4]C. Stephen Evans provides a brief response to this objection in *Philosophy of Religion* (Downers Grove, Ill.: InterVarsity Press, 1985), pp. 69-71.

[5]James Rachels lists this example along with others in *The Elements of Moral Philosophy*, 2nd ed. (New York: McGraw-Hill, 1986), pp. 15-26. His analysis is enlightening.

[6]Rachels explains this argument along with a careful analysis in *Elements of Moral Philosophy*, pp. 18-20.

[7]I refer the reader to A. C. Ewing's very thoughtful discussion of this question in *The Definition of Good* (New York: Macmillan, 1947), pp. 4-35.

Chapter 7: Morals Without God

[1]Even David Hume, who provides a major challenge to the principle of "causality," does not actually disprove it but only shows that it is not a provable concept. He also admits that in day-to-day living we must act as though this principle were operative. His challenge is in *A Treatise of Human Nature*, ed. L. A. Selby-Bigge (Oxford: Clarendon, 1967), pp. 73-84 (bk. 1, pt. 2, sec. 2-4).

[2]This is Kai Neilson's argument for a foundation for moral value in *Ethics Without God* (Buffalo: Prometheus, 1990), pp. 113-27.

[3]Peter Singer argues this in *Practical Ethics* (Cambridge: Cambridge University Press, 1981), pp. 48-71. This has proved to be a highly influential and controversial argument. The controversy itself illustrates the point I am making—namely, that there is not universal agreement on which features or characteristics give a being a right to equal or decent treatment. It is possible to construct coherent yet conflicting moral positions on both human and animal rights, depending on which features are taken to give special rights.

[4]This is a traditional viewpoint in the Western world and is usually brought out when we highlight certain abilities that humans have but animals do not. These abilities, then, become the basis for greater rights for humans.

[5]This argument is made by Paul W. Taylor, *Respect for Nature: A Theory of Environmental Ethics* (Princeton, N.J.: Princeton University Press, 1986), pp. 99-168, but particularly pp. 129-68. He labels his view a "biocentric outlook on nature." He argues specifically that the fact that humans are different from plants and other animals, due to certain capacities they have which other living things lack, does not prove superiority over them. There are, he thinks, no grounds for such a claim. After all, many nonhuman species have capacities that humans lack. He cites as examples the speed of a cheetah, the flight of birds, the power of photosynthesis in leaves, and others.

Chapter 8: Can We Be the Basis of Morals?

[1]For a helpful exposition of Christian humanism, I recommend J. I. Packer and Thomas Howard, *Christianity: The True Humanism* (Waco, Tex.: Word, 1985). Chapter 1 explains secular humanism, and the remainder of the book contrasts it with Christian humanism. The appendix includes the Christian humanist manifesto.

[2]Herbert Feigl sets out this foundation for morals in "A Dialogue on Validation and Vindication," in *Readings in Ethical Theory*, ed. Wilfred Sellars and John Hospers (Englewood Cliffs, N.J.: Appleton-Century-Crofts, 1952). See also David P. Gauthier, "Morality and Advantage," *Philosophical Review* 76 (1967): 460-75. The view Gauthier addresses would more accurately be described as the human need view, which I will turn to in the following chapter. However, there seems to be overlap in that some of his statements concern human nature and not just human needs.

[3]See Peter Singer, *Animal Liberation* (New York: New York Review, 1975), pp. 1-22.
[4]See David Hume, *A Treatise of Human Nature*, ed. L. A. Selby-Bigge, 3rd rev. ed. by P. H. Nidditch (Oxford: Oxford University Press, 1978), pp. 458, 468-70. For further reading on the fact-value problem, I recommend Tom L. Beauchamp, *Philosophical Ethics* (New York: McGraw-Hill, 1982), pp. 345-52, and William Frankena in *Perspectives on Morality*, ed. K. E. Goodpaster (Notre Dame, Ind.: University of Notre Dame Press, 1976), pp. 1-11, 133-47.

Chapter 9: Can Our Needs Be the Basis of Morals?
[1]For a proponent of this view, see John Hartland-Swan in *An Analysis of Morals* (London: George Allen & Unwin, 1960), pp. 57-61. Swan argues that what is moral or immoral depends strictly on how strongly a society feels it needs an action to be performed or avoided for its own survival or well-being. He defines morality as "the term or concept which refers to the keeping or violating of customs considered socially important—important in the mutual relations between man and man and between a man and his community."

David P. Gauthier also argues this view in "Morality and Advantage," *Philosophical Review* 76 (1967): 460-75. For a fuller treatment of social contractarianism by a number of authors, including Gauthier, see Peter Vallentyne, ed., *Contractarianism and Rational Choice: Essays on David Gauthier's Morals by Agreement* (New York: Cambridge University Press, 1991), pp. 15-95.

[2]For a more complete definition of objective versus subjective morality, see the second half of chapter one and the notes there.
[3]This is precisely Hartland-Swan's argument in *Analysis of Morals*, p. 61.
[4]This problem with the atheist's coherence explanation is set forth in the last part of chapter four.
[5]The fact-value problem, sometimes called the is-ought problem or the naturalistic fallacy, is explained in the last half of chapter eight.

Chapter 10: Morals: The Key to Survival
[1]For a better understanding of the theory of evolution, I recommend Charles Darwin, *The Origin of Species* (numerous editions are available). Michael Ruse defends the theory of evolution in *Darwinism Defended: A Guide to the Evolution Controversies* (London: Addison-Wesley, 1982). For a critical treatment, see James F. Coppedge, *Evolution: Possible or Impossible?* (Grand Rapids, Mich.: Eerdmans, 1973).
[2]This argument is made by Michael Ruse in "Is Rape Wrong on Andromeda?" in *Extraterrestrials*, ed. E. Regis Jr. (Cambridge: Cambridge University Press, 1985), pp. 60-67. For more general discussions of the relationship of evolution to ethics, see Arthur L. Caplan and Bruce Jennings, eds., *Darwin, Marx and Freud: Their Influence on Moral Theory* (New York: Plenum, 1984), especially pp. 3-69.
[3]James Q. Wilson develops this argument in his book *The Moral Sense* (New York: Free Press, 1993). For an essay adapted from this book, see "What Is Moral, and How Do We Know It?" *Commentary* 95 (June 1993): 37-43.
[4]Ruse makes this statement on p. 67 of "Is Rape Wrong on Andromeda?"

Chapter 11: Introducing God
[1]The claim contained in this paragraph is articulated often by William Lane Craig, Michael Horner and others in debates and lectures on various university campuses. Their contention is that since there are obviously moral values in the world, something more than merely the material universe must exist to account for those values.

[2]J. L. Mackie, *Miracle of Theism* (Oxford: Clarendon, 1982), p. 115.

[3]Russell argued this in *Religion and Science* (New York: Henry Holt, 1935), pp. 229-43.

[4]Fyodor Dostoyevsky, *The Brothers Karamazov*, trans. C. Garnett (New York: Signet Classics, 1957), bk. 2, chap. 6; bk. 5, chap. 5; bk. 11, chap. 8.

Chapter 12: Objecting to God

[1]See Plato's *Euthyphro* (6d-10a) for this discussion. Euthyphro and Socrates are discussing the question of what ultimately makes something right. Euthyphro suggests, in effect, that what does so is the fact that God commands it. Socrates then asks him whether something is right because God commands it or whether God commands it because it is right. For a further explanation of the Euthyphro problem with a few brief responses and counter-responses, see William K. Frankena, *Ethics*, 2nd ed. (Englewood Cliffs, N.J.: Prentice-Hall, 1973), pp. 28-30. For a brief but helpful statement of and response to the same problem, see J. P. Moreland, *Scaling the Secular City* (Grand Rapids, Mich.: Baker Book House, 1987), p. 129.